A.T.A.P
How to Achieve a Workable Classroom Environment

A.T.A.P
How to Achieve a Workable Classroom Environment

❖

In a Core Curriculum Classroom
(Grades Pre-K Through
8th and Special Education)
(A Book of Strategies and Research)

Dr. Mavis A. Bouie

Copyright © 2018 by Dr. Mavis A. Bouie.

Library of Congress Control Number:	2018908445
ISBN: Hardcover	978-1-9845-4094-2
Softcover	978-1-9845-4093-5
eBook	978-1-9845-4092-8

All rights reserved. No part of this book may be reproduced or transmitted in any form or by any means, electronic or mechanical, including photocopying, recording, or by any information storage and retrieval system, without permission in writing from the copyright owner.

The views expressed in this work are solely those of the author and do not necessarily reflect the views of the publisher, and the publisher hereby disclaims any responsibility for them.

Any people depicted in stock imagery provided by Getty Images are models, and such images are being used for illustrative purposes only.
Certain stock imagery © Getty Images.

Print information available on the last page.

Rev. date: 08/07/2018

To order additional copies of this book, contact:
Xlibris
1-888-795-4274
www.Xlibris.com
Orders@Xlibris.com

Contents

Acknowledgments ix
Introduction xi

Chapter 1: Establishing a Workable Classroom Environment 1
   Establishing Teacher Leadership 2
   Different Styles of Leadership 3
      Democratic 3
      Authoritarian 4
      Laissez-Faire 4
   Leadership Styles and Personalities 5
   Classroom Environment 6
   Arranging Your Classroom 6
   Seating Space 7
   Setting Rules and Consequences 9
   Be Consistent 10
   Overplan with Creative Activities 10

Chapter 2: Take a Personal Interest in Your Students 12
   Motivation 12
   Intrinsic motivation 13
   Extrinsic motivation 13
   Strategies That Will Motivate a Workable Classroom
   Environment 13
      • Nurture self-esteem 13
      • Set high expectations 14
      • Teacher involvement 14
      • Model a desirable behavior 15
      • Initiate an encouraging environment 15
      • Use differentiated learning 16
      • Classroom anxiety 16

Chapter 3: Teaching Procedures 18
Arriving and Leaving Class 18
Handling Classroom Rules and Procedures 18
Posting Rules and Procedures 19
Voice Levels 19
- Voice level 1 19
- Voice level 2 19
- Voice level 3 19

When the tardy bell rings 20
When the dismissal bell rings 20

Chapter 4: Resolving Classroom Conflicts: Strategies That Work 22
Don't You Deserve Respect? 25
Hitting or Threatening Teachers 26
Reflective Behavior 27
One, Two, Three. I Am Thinking. Look at Me 28
The Nonstopper 29
Workable Diversity Strategies 29

Chapter 5: Time Is a Virtue. Why Waste It? 32
Time on Task 32
Early finishers 32
Time on discipline, not on task 32
Using a timer 33
Classroom transitions 33
Promote energetic group work 33
Restless learners 33
Now, you owe me time! 34
Improve individual bathroom breaks 34
Quizzes, tests, drills 34
Slow workers 35
Students Have Too Much Spare Time 35
- Testing 35
- The start of the day and changing classes 35
- Viewing films and computer use 35
- Procedures and routines 35

Now, Who's Off Task? 36

Chapter 6: Setting Limits: Introduction 37
   Classroom Limits That Are Workable 37
   Classroom Mumbo Jumbo to Stay Away From 38
   The Ripple Effect..39
   The First Day: Let's Get Started...39
      Establish Procedures 39
      Utilize an Effective Management System 40
      Create Classroom Rules 41
      Implement a Quiet Signal..41
      Implement a Stop Strategy 41
      Raffle Ticket Strategy 42
   What Are You Thinking? Don't Put Them Down! Don't
   Criticize!..42
   When Am I Going to Get Paid? 44

Chapter 7: Models of Discipline..46
   Canter Model..46
   Glasser Model 47
   Kounin Model..48
   Behavior Modification 49
   Logical Consequences Model 50
   Teacher Effectiveness Training 51

Chapter 8: Nonverbal Messages 53
   Nonverbal Signals 54
   Facial Expression..54
   Body Language 55

Chapter 9: Parents, I Need Your Help!..57
   Classroom Strategies 57

Chapter 10: Management Course of Action 60
   Strategies 60

Chapter 11: Preschool, Two- to Four-Year-Olds.................................65
   Anything Could Happen...65
   Setting Consequences 66
   Handling Tantrums...67

Oppositional Behavior 67
Set perimeters 69
Give reminders..69
Encouragement...69
Teacher-and-Student Conference 70
Tips to Achieve an Enriched Classroom Environment............70

Free Resources..73
Summary : Let's Sum It Up!..75
Appendix...77
Glossary...79
Resources 81

ACKNOWLEDGMENTS

I would like to first acknowledge God for his divine wisdom and knowledge and those who motivated me to pursue my dreams to its fullest potentials, as well as the dedicated professors at Argosy University–Sarasota, Florida; Central Michigan University; Southern University at New Orleans; and Grand Canyon University for their expertise, knowledge, and training in education, which provided me with the essential tools to become an effective educator and researcher. Furthermore, I would like to thank the teachers from DeKalb County public schools and Atlanta public schools, Georgia, for their assistance with various drafts and annotations of the chapters. I am thankful for the encouragement from family members and friends throughout this project and to all those who believed in my dream.

Introduction

Respect and setting high expectations are essential for classroom management that should be exemplified throughout the elementary, middle, and high school environment. Students should be required to show respect to teachers, peers, and themselves. Likewise, in return, teachers should show students that same respect. In fact, in the primary grades, students thrive on structure because rules put them at ease. They know what to expect, and they are eager to please their teachers. But do not underestimate their age; they do not want to be treated as babies.

This is a book about discipline strategies that will help any educator achieve a workable classroom environment. In fact, to become an effective teacher, one must first become an effective classroom manager (Duke, 1979). By accomplishing this goal, it is important to ask yourself if you can get students to cooperate in a task the very first time they are told or carry out the classroom procedures smoothly. If you answer yes to this goal, then you are no doubt an effective classroom manager. However, many teachers have trouble with this aspect of teaching fundamentals.

Ask any novice teacher, and they will all say to you the same thing. The solution to having a successful classroom is having good classroom management. In any event, developing an effective classroom management plan is not an overnight process, but by using the tips along with strategies in this book, you can start managing a workable solution to an effective classroom environment that is conducive to good classroom management.

CHAPTER ONE

Establishing a Workable Classroom Environment

The chief fundamental to classroom management is teacher leadership and creating a learning environment that is beneficial for all learners. Therefore, it is important for the teacher to provide students with a positive social, intellectual, and physical learning environment that is appropriate for that age group. There's no doubt that this, in turn, requires that the teacher possess the ability to communicate effectively and convey an energized state of mind that would stimulate students' learning.

Research in the 1980s demonstrated that classroom management and instruction are not separate but are entwined in nature. The easiest way to explain the correlation is to look at it from a student's point of view. Research states that students, for the most part, are given two cognitive demands, which cannot be separated. These are academic task demands (understanding and working with subject matter) and social task demands (working together with others concerning that subject matter). This means that students must, at the same time, work at understanding the subject matter and find appropriate and effective ways to participate to demonstrate that understanding. Therefore, it is the teacher's responsibility to facilitate the learning of these academic and social tasks through an effective classroom management plan. Thus, from the perspective of what students need to know to be successful, management and instruction cannot be separated.

Although discipline is another concern when looking at classroom management, it should not be associated with punishment. As we observe punishment as a reaction to a disruptive behavior, discipline is concerned with the avoidance of the disruptive behavior as well as the reaction to it. For this purpose, the discipline consequence should focus on what you do to avoid the behavior as well as what you can do when a discipline problem occurs. Therefore, as a classroom teacher, it is imperative that you are knowledgeable in how to prevent a classroom disruption and an unpleasant reaction to the repercussion of the aspect of the discipline problem.

Nevertheless, when managing a classroom, one must take under consideration the three major components: a teacher that must have teacher leadership, a classroom atmosphere that is conducive to learning, and control of classroom discipline. Now, let's look at each of these components in the following sections.

Establishing Teacher Leadership

In order for teachers to maintain a workable learning environment, students must be keenly supervised. According to classroom management research, active monitoring consists of watching student behavior closely, intervening to correct unacceptable behavior before it escalates, dealing consistently with unacceptable behavior, and monitoring student learning. In terms of monitoring both student behavior and learning, effective managers regularly survey their class or group and watch for signs of student confusion or inattention. Therefore, sustaining a workable environment involves keeping an eye out for when students appear to be stuck, when they need help, when they need redirection, when they need correction, and when they need encouragement. Keeping these strategies in mind will help teachers establish a workable classroom environment.

Different Styles of Leadership

Have you ever listed the characteristics that make up a leader? Well, what type of person are you? What makes you the person you are? Are you a warm or caring person? Are you demanding, harsh, or critical? Or are you permissive or dominating? These are just a few of the characteristics inside of us that influence our leadership abilities. No matter what kind of leader you intend to become, whether you are a democratic, authoritarian, or laissez-faire leader, your leadership style will be determined by your personal characteristics. There are also other factors that will influence your leadership style, which are your school board policies, the grade or subjects, and the teacher responsibilities you have within the school organization. However, your leadership styles will change as you are assigned to other leadership responsibilities. Now, let's look at the leadership styles.

Democratic

A democratic approach to leadership is sharing the responsibility. This obtains satisfaction through others who encourage success rather than demand it. For this purpose, democratic leadership in a teacher should seek to inspire others by means of an internal and external method. In other words, democratic leaders try not to provoke people whose method of encouragement is to criticize or to degrade one's self-esteem, but they develop one's self-esteem by sharing responsibility. In fact, when students make mistakes and they are encouraged by their teachers and peers, they develop confidence in themselves, and as a result, the classroom atmosphere becomes a learning environment with open communication and independent learning. In any event, research has shown that productivity and students' performance soar in a well-run democratic learning environment.

Authoritarian

In the authoritarian approach, the leader is looked upon as one who demonstrates strength, power, and a controlling attitude of complete authority. As a teacher leader in the authoritarian approach, the teacher uses pressure and punishment to control her students. Though, the motive is to gain control over his/her students so that the sole decision maker is the teacher. The key points of the authoritarian teacher are to control students' behavior and to keep compliance of classroom and school rules through voice projection. In other words, the teacher uses sharp voice projection to put fear into his/her students. This is a form of forceful control to direct the student to do what is told.

According to research, this style of leadership only results in an atmosphere of hostility and generates in students a sense of powerlessness, competitiveness, high dependency, and alienation from the subject matter. The teacher creates an atmosphere in the classroom that discourages the students from taking chances, and most often, students develop low self-esteem and a defiant attitude with the teacher and their peers.

Laissez-Faire

In the laissez-faire approach, the teacher leader attitude is "Whatever!" Here the teacher is totally permissive to whatever happens in the classroom. Things just happen. The entire class is laid-back, and the teacher sometimes doesn't even have a clue, nor do the students. Everyone just does their own thing. However, this approach to teacher leadership, most of the time, will end up in total chaos. The students are out of control because they are disorganized and have no form of structured activities or learning, and for this reason, the students become frustrated, stressed, and begin to feel overwhelmed and uncertain on what is expected of them.

In any event, an abundance of classroom problems can be manageable if teachers would only take the democratic approach based on students' freedom to be creative, freedom of choice, and allowing them to be responsible. Instead of students going amok and just doing what they feel, they should be given freedom with limitations. Students need limits and guidance to become responsible leaders. Keep in mind that the limitations you give the students will depend on factors such as the grade level and the student's age. Just remember, when trying to determine how many limits to impose on your students, the rules should be like so: the younger they are, the more limits, and the older, the less limits.

Once you determine your teacher leadership style, you should set your classroom atmosphere accordingly. However, there are other physical factors that will affect the classroom environment, such as the way you have your classroom arranged, the color scheme of your classroom, the setup of the learning centers, and the way you utilize space. In fact, these things should be considered before changing the classroom atmosphere. Therefore, to better determine the characteristics of the different teacher leadership styles, the table below will help out.

Leadership Styles and Personalities

Democratic	Authoritarian	Laissez-Faire
Inspired	Hesitant	Unreliable
Responsive	Inconsiderate	Free-spirited
Passionate	Controlling	Tolerant
Cheering	Intrusive	Nonjudgmental
Facilitative	Boisterous	Open
Directing	Dominating	
Considerate	Critical	
Proud	Argumentative	
Open-minded	Firm	
Persuasive	Confident	

Classroom Environment

As a classroom teacher, you will have the full responsibility for the setting up of your classroom surroundings. It is up to the teacher to make the classroom appearance conducive to the students' learning styles. To accomplish this, the classroom should be colorful, clean, and have lots of storage for storing supplies, handing in papers, and disposing of trash. If the classroom has computers, there should be an area located in the back or side of the classroom for easy accessibility. Centers should be located throughout the classroom, as well as an area for students to reflect what they have learned. When students are actively involved throughout the day, discipline problems are at its lowest level. This kind of classroom atmosphere greatly enhances the functioning of the classroom and helps maintain a pleasant and productive working classroom environment for the students and teacher.

Other factors that should be taken into consideration are what I refer to as undesirable diversions, which are the lighting, temperature, and classroom ventilation. These diversions are factors that cause much classroom discomfort and disrupt the ability to concentrate. After all, if the classroom is stuffy or too hot or cold or if the lighting is dim or too bright, these factors are often a distraction, causing students to focus on the discomfort of the classroom environment rather than on their classwork. Therefore, it is the teacher's responsibility to make sure that these undesirable diversions are adjusted or that the proper people make the adjustments. Just keep in mind that comfort is the key to a relaxed and rewarding learning environment.

Arranging Your Classroom

How you arrange your classroom and students' desks are important aspects of classroom management. As you arrange your classroom, it is important to keep in mind that you are trying to achieve a manageable classroom that is conducive to a workable environment. Therefore, by doing this, the teacher should first review the students' previous progress reports, report cards, and accumulative notes or records indicating the student's conduct or work habits before considering permanent seating arrangements. Students' academic and behavior records are tools that should be reviewed before students enter the classroom. Students' records should be looked at as a road map to academic success as well as a guide to manage a workable classroom environment.

Still, when a student becomes disruptive, simply moving the disruptive student away from certain students or away from the group may control the unacceptable behavior. As a matter of fact, sometimes, placing a disruptive student near the teacher's desk frequently permits the teacher to give additional attention and individual backup the student is longing to have. Your classroom arrangement should reflect your leadership personality and the students' pervious and present behavior issues—just keep this in mind to make the learning environment workable for the whole class.

Seating Space

Wong, H. and Wong, R. (2008) states, "Students who face the board learn more when they are sitting in close to the board are in a collaborative seating arrangements." However, I must admit that there are no mapped-out requirements that will mandate a precise way to arrange seating in your classroom. But if teachers are required to differentiate instructions as they create a conducive seating arrangement, wouldn't it make sense for the student's seating to be arranged to differentiate the activity? Nevertheless, the seating arrangement should vary with every class and subject.

Here is an example of a group seating arrangement.

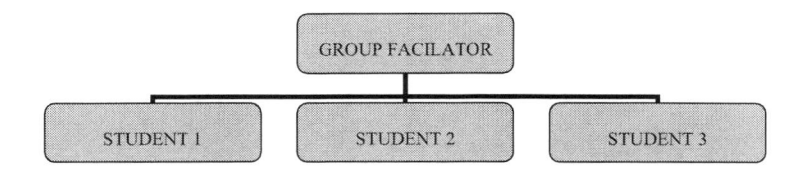

```
        ┌─────────────────┐
        │ GROUP FACILATOR │
        └────────┬────────┘
       ┌────────┼────────┐
┌──────┴──┐ ┌───┴─────┐ ┌┴────────┐
│STUDENT 1│ │STUDENT 2│ │STUDENT 3│
└─────────┘ └─────────┘ └─────────┘
```

An article written by Padmanabhan (2009) states that Nigel Hastings, professor of Nottingham Trent University, England, has been researching classroom behavior for the last twenty years. His research indicates that children work much better in seating arrangement of rows rather than sitting in groups. He believes that when students are placed in groups, they are more talkative and waste too much time from completing their classwork.

In fact, his study found that when children were made to sit by themselves or in pairs and not in groups, they were more attentive to their work, and their attentiveness increased between 16 percent and 124 percent. Also, he said that if students are observed in groups as they work on a task, the majority do not collaborate, and they work independently to complete their work.

So try this strategy in your classroom, and you will see that the most disruptive student will double their efforts to complete their work when made to sit alone to focus on the task. Research results clearly indicate that giving students an increase of physical space between desks encourages an increased time on a task and discourages disruptive behavior because students are facing the front of the class and the teacher can freely move throughout the desk space to assist and monitor students. However, from previous experiences, I believe that students are more attentive to retaining what they learn when working and collaborating in small groups.

Setting Rules and Consequences

Setting classroom rules is the most important factor when establishing a workable classroom environment. Therefore, it is essential to establish rules, consequences, and rewards on the first day of school. A set of clear and concise rules and consequences are very important. When establishing classroom rules, I find that involving students in the process makes them feel more accountable for their actions as well as helps them remember the rules.

As you assist students in brainstorming classroom rules, at the most, try to limit them to four or five. Keep in mind to encourage students to consider rules in terms of things that should be done instead of things that should not be done. For example, say, "Raise your hand before getting out of your seat" instead of "Do not get out of your seat without permission." Or say, "Keep hands, feet, and objects to yourself" instead of "Do not throw objects or touch others." Lastly, say, "Walk quietly in the hallway" instead of "Talking in the hallway is unacceptable." Just remember that rules should always be clear and easily understood by students. Also, have rules posted in an area in the classroom that is visible at eye height.

When brainstorming consequences, encourage appropriate ideas for that age group and make sure to process the consequences as the behavior develops. In fact, placing the student on a behavior modification chart or checklist is an excellent strategy to consider. In addition, have a "visual" for students to focus on or to write the infraction. For example, a bulletin board, notebook, index box with index cards, or Rolodex are only a few tools to consider when documenting classroom behavior.

Nevertheless, when the infraction is serious, it is important to bypass the first or second consequences and proceed to a more decisive result. Also, at the same time, it is just as important to have established rewards and display of these rewards as a visible motivation for acceptable classroom behavior. In any event, the most valuable strategy to managing students' classroom behavior so that the student will become workable is parental contact. Yes, staying in contact with the parent and developing a powerful, workable relationship is very important when managing your classroom. However, you must set limitations on parental contact so that you will not appear to be a nuisance. Use all your school resources such as other teachers and administrators, have a conference with the student and have him/her brainstorm consequences and rules just for that individual student, most of all, research for similar problems for a solution. Oh, don't forget to *document everything*!

Be Consistent

From my teaching experience, I realize that the worst thing to do is to not be consistent when enforcing class rules. When you enforce your rules one day and disregard the rules the next day, your students will receive mixed messages, which indicate that the rules are just not that important and you are simply telling them that it is okay to break the rules. Keep in mind that enforcing the rules later will be much more difficult to do if you don't enforce it when the disruption occurs. Be consistent and fair-minded, and remember that the same punishment should pertain for the same rule for all students.

Overplan with Creative Activities

One of the primary reasons why teachers are having classroom disruptions is that students are not engaging in an ongoing variety of classroom activities. It is very important to have enough activities that are differentiated with the students' learning styles. For example, have files and folders of activities that will cover almost all learning skills and subjects. Teacher-made games are the best because you can design a game on the skills presently being taught. Another excellent strategy is to let the students create games on learned skills. They will enjoy doing this as well as teaching the game to other students. Make sure that the lessons you are engaging the students in are interesting, challenging, and on grade level. However, you still need to consider creating activities for gifted and inclusion students. I would suggest having a variety of centers such as reading/writing/social studies, phonics/grammar, listening (cassette story tapes, Language Master), math/science, and technology. By doing this, you will be able to accommodate the needs of all students. It is best to have more than enough activities because if you don't, you will leave students with leisure time, which will lead to classroom disruptions.

Chapter Two

Take a Personal Interest in Your Students

It is important for students to know that you care and are interested in their academic success. So try to show that you are interested in what they have to say. Talk to your students, and most of all, listen. However, don't say anything that would put you in jeopardy of your job. Don't say anything that could be taken by the student as negative. When talking to your students, it might be a good idea to try to think as a child before you speak because they usually hear what they want to hear. Always ask them to explain what you just said. This strategy will help clarify any misunderstanding by the student. In addition, try to speak to each child about something other than schoolwork. This could be a challenge, but it is not impossible. You can begin this strategy as a morning routine. Say simple comments like, "I like your hairstyle," "You have on a neat outfit," "Good morning," or "How is it going today?" This is an excellent approach to let the students know that you are interested and you care.

Motivation

According to research and the Wikipedia Online Encyclopedia (2002), educational psychologists are particularly interested in motivation and what role it plays in student learning. However, the kind of motivation that is studied in the education setting is different in research from the more general forms of motivation studied by psychologists in other fields.

Motivation in education can have several effects on how students learn and how they behave toward subject matters. Wikipedia also states that motivation can

1. direct behavior toward goals,
2. lead to increased effort and energy,
3. increase initiation of and persistence in activities,
4. enhance cognitive processing,
5. determine what consequences are reinforcing, and
6. lead to improved performance.

In fact, students are not always internally motivated; they sometimes need position motivation, which is found in environmental conditions that are created by the teacher. Research states and defines two kinds of motivation:

- <u>Intrinsic motivation</u> occurs when people are internally motivated to do something because it either brings them pleasure, they think it is important, or they feel that what they are learning is significant. (Wikipedia, 2002)
- <u>Extrinsic motivation</u> comes into play when a student is compelled to do something or act a certain way because of factors external to him or her such as money or good grades. (Wikipedia, 2002)

Strategies That Will Motivate a Workable Classroom Environment

- *Nurture self-esteem.* Give classwork so that all students will achieve success. Therefore, it is important to make sure that classwork is differentiated according to the student's learning

style and abilities. Keep in mind that repeated failure will result in the attitude to stop trying.
- *Set high expectations.* Brehm and Kassin's (1996), Benard's (1995), Jussim and Eccles's (1992) research reveal that students tend to live up to their *teacher's* expectations. Therefore, teacher expectations then can be used to motivate students. For this purpose, teachers can expect and demand the students' best efforts in classwork. Also, it is important for teachers to share goals, objectives, and procedures on attaining what is expected of them. By doing this, students need to be involved in developing class goals, objectives, and procedures. They need to be aware of what is to be expected, where they are going, and how they are going to get there. In any event, sharing expectations gives students a sense of responsibility for their own actions and a sense of accomplishment when they reach goals and objectives.
- *Teacher involvement.* Students tend to get excited when their teacher gets actively involved in group or class activities. Remember the theory of conservation energy as stated in Wikipedia (2002), p. 4. *He says that, "it is true."*

> the total amount of energy in an isolated system remains constant. The consequence of this law is that energy cannot be created or destroyed. However, the only thing that can happen with energy in an isolate system is that it can change its form. For example, kinetic energy can become thermal energy. In other words, based on Einstein's theory of relativity, energy cannot be change or transfer unless, another source of energy is permitted to enter or leave the system.

Therefore, looking at this theory from an educator's point of view, if a teacher enters the classroom with a frond of frustration caused from a ghastly morning commute to school, the negative attitude (energy) observed in the teacher's facial expression or tone of voice by the students can be rippled down to students through the teacher's oral directions for morning assignments. This is the reason why teachers sometimes observe negative attitudes from students at the start of the day and vice versa. The students' negative attitude (energy) may ripple down to the teacher as well. Therefore, it is so important for teachers to establish positive attitudes at the start of the school day and continue it throughout the course of the day. So keep in mind that these strategies will help avoid ripple effects of negative behavior from students to teacher and from teacher to students. In addition, teachers will see students becoming more receptive without attitudes and be involved with activities rather than being off task and talking to their friends.

- *Model a desirable behavior.* When teachers teach through examples, they are teaching students how to model. For this reason, if students follow the teacher's examples, students will eventually change their behavior. In fact, when the teacher shows enthusiasm about an activity or subject, the students will show enthusiasm. Keep in mind that enthusiasm can be very contagious as well as an enriching and rewarding learning experience.
- *Initiate an encouraging environment.* Start off the school year by sharing the fact that all students have an important job. Keep students actively involved through questioning, sharing, and collaborating ideas. Use this time to brainstorm with students' incentives for appropriate behavior. Just communicating the importance of every lesson and activity will make students' learning a meaningful experience. Still keep in mind that the students' self-esteem must be cultivated so that they can feel important and respected. Therefore, plan all assignments so that all students will accomplish success. Research states that if students have repeated failures, they will soon have the

desire to stop trying. Therefore, for this reason, you'll want to keep encouraging students to achieve set goals.

- *Use differentiated learning.* This is sometimes referred as differentiated instruction. It is a plan that uses a variety of instructional strategies that address students' learning needs. The goals of differentiated learning is to develop challenging and engaging tasks for each learner (from low-end learners to high-end learners). Instructional activities are flexible and based on content areas in reading, language, math, science, and social studies. Teachers respond to students' readiness, instructional needs, interests, and the best way for learners to learn. Learners are also provided with opportunities to work in varied instructional formats. In a nutshell, a differentiated learning environment is a learner-responsive, teacher-facilitated classroom where all students can meet curriculum objectives within an environment that is conducive to their learning style (Wikipedia, 2002).

  As a result, differentiated learning will make the student feel in control, responsible in completing assignments, as well as successful at the assigned task.

- *Classroom anxiety.* When students are nervous and feel discomfort in class, most likely they will have trouble becoming successful learners. So to reduce the discomfort, teachers need to be careful when handing out assignments and exams that are unrealistic to complete. Having a workable classroom environment requires that students can attain goals and objectives that are reachable. If the assignments are too hard for the students to complete, inappropriate behavior will occur.

Motivating students is not an easy task. However, the strategies in this book will help you begin developing and evaluating your techniques for motivating your students. Keep in mind that classroom motivation is a valuable tool that will help you develop a workable classroom environment that is conducive for all learners.

> Children need guidance in and out of the classroom. So let's delight in the joy of giving them our best. Their growth in learning how to handle situations are the foundations of making wise choices and decisions.
>
> —Dr. Mavis Bouie

CHAPTER THREE

Teaching Procedures

Arriving and Leaving Class

When students arrive at school in the morning, they are most likely still sleepy, grumpy, and a little melancholy. Therefore, it is very important for the teacher to greet students at the door with a smile and encouraging words, as well as at the end of the day. Your encouraging words might be the only positive adult support the student has all day. Be aware of your students' moods in the morning. A kind word or two, such as "I like your outfit," "Your hair looks great," or "I am glad you are at school today," just might be all that he/she needs to hear to redirect a negative attitude to a positive one. To set the learning tempo, students need to see their teacher model positive behavior at the start and end of the school day.

Handling Classroom Rules and Procedures

Teaching classroom procedures and rules is not an easy task to accomplish, but it is just as important as modeling behavior. When teaching rules and procedures, it is very important to spend a lot of time practicing and reinforcing them. In fact, it is imperative to reinforce and practice repeatedly during the first month of school.

The same applies to middle school and high school students; just keep in mind that these students attend other classes with teachers. Therefore, the other teachers' rules and procedures may be different from yours. In addition, at the beginning of the school year, it might be advantageous to inquire with the other teachers concerning their classroom rules and procedures. It is important that all teachers' classroom rules and procedures are consistent.

Posting Rules and Procedures

Make sure that when posting procedures and rules, they are located at the front of the classroom. You want this to be the focal point of your classroom environment.

Voice Levels

There are different levels of voice we use in school versus our outside voice. Teachers should not expect students to make the transition if they are not taught the difference. It is up to you to explain the different voice levels and model to your students, *thus the addition for the following*:

- *Voice level 1.* This level is the low voice tone when you are speaking in a whisper to the person sitting next to you.
- *Voice level 2.* The natural medium voice projection to someone sitting across the dinner table.
- *Voice level 3.* The outside loud voice used on the playground or outdoors.

The best way to demonstrate voice levels is to turn up the volume on a radio, CD player, or TV to low, medium, and loud volume. Then, explain during the demonstrations what sound pitch is acceptable or unacceptable in your classroom and throughout the school. Next, list them to influence the importance. Then post voice-level rules for walking in the hallways, restroom, and your classroom. Remember, you are trying to establish a workable environment without noise pollution. Managing your students' voice level behaviors isn't just in your classroom; it is in every perimeter of the school.

Paula Naegle (2002), in her article "Teaching Routines and Classroom Procedures," suggest a few ideas of high school procedures.

When the tardy bell rings, the following should be done:

1. Be in your seat and ready to work quietly.
2. Place your homework assignment on your desk so it is ready to be collected
3. Begin the opening activity (directions are on the board/overhead projector each day).
4. Wait quietly for the teacher's instruction.

When the dismissal bell rings, the following should be done:

1. At the sound of the bell, close your book and stop working.
2. Stay in your seat until you hear the teacher dismiss you.
3. Leave quietly and in an orderly manner.

If I Only Knew
If I only knew what is expected of me, I
could be whatever I want to be.
If I only had someone to show me the ways,
I could better my inner abilities.
If you only could hear the plea of my heart, crying out to help me
because I am lost in the darkness of my ways and my thoughts.
So don't look at me and think I just know, because
I won't if you never took the time to tell me so.

— Dr. Mavis A. Bouie

Chapter Four

Resolving Classroom Conflicts: Strategies That Work

Resolving conflict in the classroom has become a top priority for teachers and school administrators to ensure the safety of the students and facility. With the right strategy, teachers have found that most conflicts can be resolved in a quick and simple manner. Here are some strategies to use when faced with conflict situations.

First, be specific when defining the problem in writing or verbally and always give each student a chance to share their feelings. Second, brainstorm possible solutions that will satisfy everyone. When doing this, it might be a good idea to list the ideas. Third, all should agree on one solution that makes sense to both parties. Make sure that students understand that sometimes when you agree to a solution, the product of the solution might not always be what you expect. For example, the students may have been friends, and because of the problem, the solution might cause them to stay away from each other. This solution may cause one or the other to lose trust in the friendship. Fourth, implement the solution, and lastly, decide together if the problem has been resolved. If not, continue to brainstorm other alternative solutions.

Sometimes, it might take removing the student(s) to another area of the classroom or another teacher's room for a few minutes. However, when moving the student out of the classroom, remember that it is still your responsibility to retrieve your student. I would suggest giving the student ten minutes of breathing time and then retrieve him/her from the other class. Also, when sending a student to another teacher's classroom, always send classwork with the student. Only use this strategy as a last result. However, do not make it a habit to send your student out of the class because students will use this strategy just to get out of the classroom.

Once the student has returned to the class, set them aside to confer with the student and email or phone the parent and document the infraction. If the behavior continues more than three times, request a parent conference to have the student placed on a daily behavior chart to monitor conduct and work habits. I find that using a daily behavior chart is an excellent way to keep the parent(s) informed on how their child is progressing or digressing in classroom work habits and conduct. Keep in mind to *nip* (stop) unacceptable behavior right in its tracks. Handle the problem immediately by making the student aware that a classroom rule or rules were broken. Just do not ignore the problem. That's a bad mistake!

When telling students how to act in class, it is important for teachers to be specific and to use positive communication. Do not assume that students are aware of what good behavior looks like. In fact, it is the teacher's responsibility to model the type of behavior the teacher is trying to establish. For instance, if students were never shown a straight line, how do expect them to line up in a straight line? What about the high school students not being respectful during instruction? Well, it is a possibility that respect was never expressed to students, so why would you expect students to react to what you are saying in a positive way? Therefore, how teachers and parents model their behaviors will reflect on how students behave in and out of the classroom setting.

Suzanne Pitner (2009) states in her article "Positive Classroom Discipline: Teacher Strategies That Encourage Responsive Students" that "positive discipline includes positive language." The teacher sets the tone of the classroom, and by focusing on specific, clear instructions with a positive overtone, the students will respond accordingly. Rather than telling a student who is drawing instead of reading that she is not doing what she is supposed to do, tell the student, "It's time to put the pencil away and open your book." Another way is to tell the student, "It's reading time now. Please put the pencil down and read." As mentioned earlier, a positive overtone when speaking to students will give them a sense of authority with respect in your voice. Students hear the seriousness and will respond in a positive manner. However, every student and class is different. Therefore, it is important to set high expectations and your authority at the beginning of the school year and continue to maintain your expectations all year.

Instead of focusing on what the student is doing wrong, let's take a minute and focus on what the student is doing right. For example, a middle school or high school student is reading a book in class and tapping on his/her desk. The tapping noise is disturbing the other students. Instead of correcting the student's negative behavior (tapping), let's focus on what the student is doing correct. Therefore, when correcting the unwanted behavior, say to the student, "I like the way you are working very quietly. Keep up the good work." This will indirectly make the student aware that you notice that he/she is doing a good job reading quietly but that tapping on the desk is unacceptable behavior. As a result, your positive comment will redirect the negative behavior to a positive one, and the student's awareness of the tapping on the desk will stop. This concept is somewhat based on Lee Canter's perspective, which indicates that teachers should not try to catch students doing something wrong and discipline them for it. Instead, teachers and students should work together to establish good behavior that would last throughout the school year.

When students engage in minor misbehavior, it is important to use a calm verbal reprimand when speaking to them. In other words, it is not what you say to students that make them become aggressive, but it is how it sounds to them when you speak. For example, one of your classroom rules might be to raise your hand if you have a question or comment during lectures. If a few students begin whispering during a lecture, you might walk over to them and say, "Keep in mind, if you have something to say during a lecture, you are supposed to raise your hand and wait to be called on. Therefore, if you do not wish to share your thoughts with the class, you should not be talking." It is most critical that a calm verbal reprimand be delivered peacefully and gently because showing anger weakens the process. In fact, the way you approach the students should imply that they probably did not fully understand your expectations. Therefore, from that point on, this is the opportunity to redirect students' behavior by reiterating direct information so that their classroom demeanor can improve.

By using this strategy, it will reduce the likelihood that students will resent being reprimanded, and they will not challenge your authority to save face with their peers. However, handle the verbal reprimand as quickly as possible, but never involve the entire class during the process. On the other hand, keep in mind that immediacy should not be sacrificed for privacy, because if you wait until the end of the instructional period to reprimand a student, your actions will imply to the other students that the inappropriate behavior is acceptable. So do not jeopardize classroom control by taking the student into the hallway to reprimand them. This will cause loss of immediacy, and the interruption could prompt other behavioral problems while you are out of the room. Immediate verbal reprimands are most successful when the teacher walks over to the student or students and quietly tells them how they need to improve their behavior. In any event, the only disadvantage when using a verbal reprimand is, it is a short-term intervention. Therefore, if the unacceptable behavior continues after you have used verbal reprimand several times, you will need to change your strategy.

Don't You Deserve Respect?

What do you do when a student gives you the finger in class? Do you send him to the principal's office? However, during the adventure and enjoyable stay in the principal's office, at no time is the student told that what he did was wrong, but instead, they're told that it was inappropriate. Now thirty minutes later, the student is back in your class, ruining the education of the other students. Later, the student's mother is contacted, and she comes down to the school or phone and angrily demands of the principal, "What did your teacher do to make my child give her the middle finger?" How would you handle this scenario with the student?

The first thing is to not look upset. Immediately let the student know that kind of behavior is unacceptable. Showing anger will only escalate the behavior. So with that in mind, direct the reprimand to the class by saying, "Class, was the behavior of your classmate appropriate? What is our class motto? Yes, our class motto is to *respect*. Therefore, to receive respect, we must give respect. For that reason, you should respect your teacher always. Now, Johnny has broken the rule and disrespected all of us. Therefore, he should apologize to all of us." Using this strategy will redirect the students' attention to Johnny and not Johnny giving the teacher the finger. The students will feel that they, too, are victims of Johnny's behavior and expect him to apologize to them as well. This strategy is plain, old, simple positive peer pressure. As for the parent, I would let the principal handle it because at that point, the parent really doesn't want to speak with the teacher.

Hitting or Threatening Teachers

A student hitting a teacher is a serious incident that warrants a serious reaction, and not responding to it can dramatically alter the atmosphere of the classroom. Therefore, it is necessary for the teacher to be able to react to the incident safely and effective. According to an article by Dr. Ken Shore, "Being struck or threatened by a student can undermine a teacher's authority—especially if the teacher loses control when reacting to the experience—and it can frighten other students. Teachers have an opportunity through their handling of such a situation to demonstrate their authority and control, and to restore a sense of security and calm among students." Therefore, when responding, it is important to keep in mind the nature of the incident, student's age, and the intent because there is a difference between a student who is three to five years old who is experiencing a tantrum, swaying his/her arms, and hitting the teacher and the twelve- to eighteen-year-old who hits a teacher with the intent to harm. The same motives pertain to students who imply threats to teachers. Remember that all threats should be responded to; however, the seriousness of the incident needs to be taken into consideration as well.

An article by Dr. Shore, "Hitting or Threatening a Teacher," addresses seven strategies teachers can use when faced with this nature of behavior. These are the following:

- Respond to a student's threats even if he is unlikely to carry them out.
- Immediately let the principal know if the student's actions are perceived to be serious or if the student hits you.
- Distract the volatile student.
- Convey to the student the seriousness of his behavior.
- Use physical restraint sparingly.
- Confer with the parents.
- If student has a history of aggressive behavior, ask other teachers to be on call if student loses control.
- If concerned for your safety, request the student's removal from your class.

Reflective Behavior

On a whole, students don't see their behavior as teachers do. So when a student is being rude or just sitting in their seat improperly, try this strategy in a friendly, nonthreatening approach. Demonstrate the postures, gestures, or tone of voice the student is using. Then let the student know in a nonintimidating tone of voice and example and say, "I don't speak like that to you. The tone of voice you are using is disrespectful." Explain to the student that speaking using a negative tone of voice will sometimes make other people speak back to you in a negative or not-so-nice voice. You might also want to act out the way the student spoke. In addition, say to the unruly student, "I know that you are capable of excellent classroom behavior. However, starting today, your classmates and I want to see an improvement in your behavior. Don't we, class?" In any event, your intention is to give the student a vivid picture of the unwanted behavior that was displayed, and usually as a result, the negative will turn into a positive. Just remember to always stay calm and keep direct eye contact as you speak.

One, Two, Three. I Am Thinking. Look at Me

How many lessons have you taught where, before you could finish the introduction or give directions, one or two students would raise their hand to ask a question? Here are a few approaches that help limit interruptions and force students to listen and think about what they are going to say before you call on them to respond to questions. However, let the students know that the speaker might call on them to respond to a question during the lecture or talk.

1. Always remind the students that when someone is speaking to the class, they should give respect by listening to the speaker until the speaker finishes talking.
2. If the student's hand is raised and the speaker looks at the student (or glances) then looks away, the student should repeat in their head, "One, two, three. Look at me."
3. If the speaker has not responded at the count of three, the student should put their hand down and wait until the speaker asks, "Are there any questions?"

Establishing the "one, two, three, look at me" strategy in your listening rules and practicing it during daily group sessions will help students become more conscious of the procedures.

The Nonstopper

In every classroom, you will find at least two or three students who never stop talking. They just drive you crazy, and you find yourself spending too much energy and time telling the talkative students to "stop talking!" The tactics for these categories of students are to focus your attention on the students who are not talking. For example, say, "I like the way Khamilah is working quietly. Oh my! Khadijah is working quietly too." Another approach is to focus your attention on the two students who are talking. However, say to one of them, "When you finish talking, let me know so you can get back to your work" or "Are you explaining work to your friend? If you are, let's not forget to finish your work." Approaching a student in a nonthreatening way will eliminate or redirect the behavior in a positive direction.

Workable Diversity Strategies

To avoid multicultural issues in a diverse classroom, I would suggest encouraging parents of different cultures to volunteer at least once or twice a week to assist you in class, group activities, projects, or fieldtrips. Students will eventually become comfortable working with parents of other cultures and begin to view their classmates of different countries as a friend more quickly. In fact, I have experienced that once students become comfortable with other students of different cultures, they begin to exchange ideas and collaborate more about their individual customs. In addition, their inquisitiveness results in a lifelong learning process that leads to student research and ongoing activities and discussions.

Another strategy would be to invite parents of different cultures to give input when constructing classroom rules, projects, as well as school decisions. However, I suppose by now you are saying to yourself, "How can I do this when most of the parents do not speak English?" Well, I would suggest for your school administrators to encourage teachers to get training in the dominant languages in the school environment through in-school staff development workshops or classes offered by your school system. Also, it might be a good idea for the school administrators to survey parents of different cultures who can speak English clearly enough to teach a staff development class after school to the teachers. However, this sort of project will require a grant proposal for supplies and compensation for the lecturer (parent). Remember, your plan is to make parents of different countries feel like they are part of their child's learning experiences.

The next strategy would include parents of different countries participating in the class's cultural awareness. Parents and their children can share the diversity of their culture with other students and the teacher through a variety of stories, songs, and foods. This approach will also help students understand why some students of different cultures wear certain clothing and eat similar foods.

Furthermore, including diversity learning centers in the classroom would enrich learning to the extent that students will have the opportunity to explore hands-on activities such as diverse reading, stories, ways of learning math in other countries, and handwriting activities. In addition, a multicultural classroom library would help the students venture into a more in-depth understanding of different cultural concepts and geographic knowledge. Playing multicultural music during center or classroom downtime will also give students the opportunity to appreciate an awareness of other diverse music.

Once a week, I suggest to the class to collaborate in a circle discussion group. In the group, direct the student's attention to appreciate, through discussion, the diverse customs of students in their class through questions and answers. Brainstorm ways to handle negativity among diversity in the school and classroom. Then discuss ways to approach and eliminate the problems in a nonviolent way. Finally, have students randomly select a student's name from a container to research on their background culture and present it to the class in the next circle group discussion. For the younger students, I suggest that they bring in one or two facts about the cultural background and discuss the findings as a whole group.

Through research and collaboration of multicultural awareness, I believe that the outcome of the strategies I suggest will encourage non-negative attitudes among students of different cultures as well as improve parents' participation and contribute to a workable classroom environment for all students.

Chapter Five

Time Is a Virtue. Why Waste It?

Time on Task

Time on task or engaged time is different from mandated or instructional time allocated by the school region. In fact, time on task or engaged time is the actual time that each student spends on their classwork. During engaged time, students are physically and mentally participating in the learning process. The type of student participation may possibly be solving math problems, reading, writing, working in centers, or sitting quietly, listening, and taking notes as the teacher lectures. Research says that if students are not actively engaged in the learning process, they will not learn (Berliner, 1987). Below are some strategies that will help to improve a student's time on task:

Early finishers. Always keep an eye out for early finishers. Usually, when students finish their work early, they start talking to the students who are not finished or start doing just about anything to annoy the class. Therefore, you should avoid this dilemma by planning more instruction activities than you think you need. Always overplan with other enriching activities such as file folder / teacher-made games and listening activities with response worksheets.

Time on discipline, not on task. All teachers have discipline problems; however, writing discipline referrals often interrupts class instruction. So to redirect the unwanted behavior, the teacher can use nonverbal maneuvers to curb unacceptable behavior so that the lesson can proceed without further interruptions. The following are examples:

- *Using a timer.* Time management is important during classroom management. Most often, teachers have a great deal of activities and skills to cover and little time to waste. Using count and countdown timers can energize your class routine by keeping both teacher and students attentive and time conscious (time on task). Timers are not only used to maintain a student's time on task or enhance a student's learning, it can also be used to time student's on errands to the office, teacher classrooms and the school library.

Other ways to use timers

- *Classroom transitions.* Start a two-minute timer as students transition from one learning activity to another, line up at the door, move to centers, etc. Always praise students who transition successfully within the time limit.
- *Promote energetic group work.* Establish a list of questions to the class and direct students to think of a possible answer. Instruct that they may work in small or large groups. Start the five-minute countdown timer. After the minutes are up, call randomly on the students in the group.
- *Restless learners.* If students become restless and are not motivated to work, encourage them by suggesting that if they work very hard to complete their work before the timer rings, you (the teacher) will give them fifteen minutes of free time to engage in center activities or five minutes to visit with a friend in the class in a "constructive, open-ended, comprehensive questions" conversation. Start the timer for fifteen-minute countdown and begin the instructional lesson. As a result, students will be motivated to engage in the lesson because they want to earn extra time to engage in select activities for class participation and work performance. Also, students will

now be aware that the timer will allot the lesson to last for a certain length of time.

- *Now, you owe me time!* Using this strategy works every time. When students are working in a group or with partners, to achieve control of classroom behavior, say to your students, "If classroom behavior gets out of control and interferes with learning, the entire class will owe me [the teacher] for lost time on task." So before classroom behavior gets out of control, always let students know that you are setting the timer for three minutes for them to get their behavior under control. Set the timer and wait quietly. If students stop unacceptable behavior before the timer bell rings, note on the board the number of minutes and seconds that the instruction was interrupted. Repeat this sequence as often as needed during the lesson's activities. At the end of the class period or school day, add up the total amount of time lost. Then inform students that they must repay time back in the course of losing free time, having silent lunch in the cafeteria, staying after school with the teacher (make arrangements with parents), and completing work that was not finished in class.
- *Improve individual bathroom breaks.* When students ask to go to the restroom, let them know that the timer will be set to three minutes. They will have one minute to get to the restroom, one minute to take care of their personal needs, and one minute to get back to class. Let them see you start the timer, and then say, "Be back before the timer bell rings." Next, say to them, "Go!" This strategy will make the student aware of how valuable time is as well as to not play in the restroom and return to class as quickly as possible. When setting up restroom break rules, these procedures should be discussed.
- *Quizzes, tests, drills.* Timers are valuable tools to use during testing, drilling, or quizzing students. When using a timer to quiz, test, or drill students, this strategy will help condition students to be more accurate in reading and thinking before answering questions. However, when using this strategy, it

is important to keep in mind that you (the teacher) are only promoting speed and accuracy.
- *Slow workers.* Set the timer to help speed up the students' working habits as well as give extra time to complete work. Always set the timer near the student(s) to keep them time conscious. When the timer bell rings, the student should have completed his/her work.

Students Have Too Much Spare Time

If students are not engaged in learning, you are giving them the opportunity to think of what they can do to disrupt the learning atmosphere. As a matter of fact, some educators support the fact that as much as 50 to 60 percent of the school days a year are wasted on the following:

1. *Testing.* At least five to fifteen days a year are lost due to district-wide and standardized testing.
2. *The start of the day and changing classes.* At least ten to fifteen minutes per day is taken from instructional time just to take attendance, listen to announcements, and other classroom interruptions.
3. *Viewing films and computer use.* If this strategy is being used, make sure it is to compare and contrast to a story read in the class. Keep students involved with questions throughout the movie. Make sure that students are taking notes to complete compare-and-contrast worksheets with their partners at the end of the movie, as well as writing story sequences and details. Just make sure that core standards are aligned with the activities.
4. *Procedures and routines.* There are so many teachers who spend too much time on simple classroom routines and procedures. Routine and procedures should be set up in such a way that the classroom will run smoothly. For example, lining up for

lunch, going to the restroom, collecting papers, passing out papers, and sharpening pencils should be well-thought-out and simplified at the beginning of the school year or during the week of teachers' post planning by grade levels.

Therefore, if you are consistent with rules and daily procedures, your class will not be disorderly toward the end of the school year.

Now, Who's Off Task?

Recognizing when students are not engaged or are off task depends on how sharp the teacher's observation skills are. Here are some things to look out for during instructional time:

- Students are looking at you (eye contact).
- Are their hands or feet still?
- Make sure heads are not on desk.
- Check for gum, paper chewers, etc.
- Look for eye movement during seatwork engagement.

Remember to always continuously scan the perimeter of the classroom no matter what you are engaged in with students and others. Being sensitive to these indicators, as well as the ones you develop, will help you keep your students engaged and on task toward a more workable classroom environment.

Being Off Task
When students are off task, they seem to make teachers mad
But being off task might be their way to say "I am bored."
So lighten up and don't be mad when
you see your students off task.

—Dr. Mavis Bouie

Chapter Six

Setting Limits: Introduction

Who knows their students better than the teacher? Therefore, you should develop an overall approach to discipline that is appropriate for your class. Students need and want to know their limitations. They want to know what is expected of them and their role as a student. So if teachers avoid giving students and enforcing limitations, the classroom's working environment will be headed for conflict after conflict among students.

As mentioned earlier, when establishing rules, clarity and consistency are vital components. So always explain why certain rules are needed, and during the explanation brainstorm with students, give examples that would indicate a clear picture in their mind.

Classroom Limits That Are Workable

1. Students may not know what kind of behavior is unacceptable. Therefore, make clear the precise nature of what you consider to be unacceptable classroom behavior. For instance, a student should not get out of their seat during instructional time, speak out of turn or out loud, or distract others by making loud noises. If students are aware that this kind of behavior

will not be tolerated in class, then they will become more conscientious of their actions.
2. Provide students with two choices. One choice will be what you want the student to do. The other choice will be meaningful consequences such as a phone call to the parent, detention, etc. Keep in mind that the consequences must always be put into effect, as it relates to the unwanted behavior. However, be aware that there are some students who disrupt the class only to be put out or suspended. These students should not have a choice, but consequences should be dealt with according to the infraction, mandated by the school discipline policy.
3. You want the student to realize that they are in control of their behavior. Therefore, it is very important for the teacher to allow the student time to determine their consequence choices.
4. Continuously hold fast to your limits. Never be perceived as a teacher who says that you are going to enforce consequences for inappropriate behavior and never does.

Classroom Mumbo Jumbo to Stay Away From

1. Do not ever say to the student, "Do it now!" Most students react negatively when the teachers use this phrase to make them do their work.
2. Never threaten a student for any reason.
3. Always make sure the student clearly understands why the consequence is being enforced and never say to the student, "You are doing this because I said so, and you have *no say.*"
4. Never humiliate the student, and always show respect.
5. Never give students ultimatums.
6. Always remain calm and never get involved in power struggles with a student.

Using these tips will help you become more effective at dealing with unacceptable classroom behavior, and every day you will find yourself less and less stressed and loving what you do as well.

The Ripple Effect

When the teacher openly corrects or reprimands a student for inappropriate classroom behavior in the classroom, the outcome may sometimes be illustrated by a ripple effect in other students. In other words, students tend to act up when they see other classmates misbehaving. Therefore, it is so important to set the classroom tone with rules and consequences the first week of school. Never let the student think that he/she can get away with the unacceptable behavior because this will only encourage the other students to test you. Conversely, if you nip the student's inappropriate behavior in the bud when it happens by applying the rules and consequences, the implied action will ripple to the other students, and they will be less likely to provoke the teacher in an argument about their misbehavior or break that same rule in the future.

Try to avoid criticizing because it just provokes hostility in students. When students are approached and reprimanded in a negative way, they may react in a very hostile way and say something unintentional or just stop working. Putting the students down in front of their peers embarrasses them. So try to be very direct and restate the rules and consequences, and most of all, show respect when correcting students' classroom behavior.

The First Day: Let's Get Started

Establish Procedures

Drill, drill, and drill procedures daily. Do not move to any fun activities until students show you that they understand and know the classroom and school procedures. You need to make sure that your procedures are very clear and direct. Ask the students to repeat rules, procedures, and consequences. Just remember to drill daily and keep drilling until the end of the school year. Let this be a part of your morning meetings, after lunch, and the end-of-the-day closing routine.

Utilize an Effective Management System

Let your students know how important they are by conferencing with them on a weekly basis. Most school systems are monitoring students' behaviors by writing and signing in the students' agenda. The agenda is an excellent strategy; however, you need to go a little beyond just writing in the student's agenda weekly. Do things such as contacting parents through a free app. There are a host of free computer and phone apps on Microsoft or Google. Also, if you need to confer with your students' parents and have problems getting in contact with them, consult your administrators or counselors for suggestions. If you believe that a parent might be difficult to talk with, have someone on your team or administrator sit in on your conference. Just make sure that you and the other teacher(s) or administrator(s) are taking notes to confirm what was said during the conference.

Keep in mind to phone or email the parents once a week or once every two weeks. Staying in contact is your best defense. However, when you phone the parents, tell them something positive about their child before telling them something negative. In the same token, no parent wants to always hear negative comments about their child. Therefore, make sure that some of your phone calls are complimenting *good* behavior that week. Remember that parent support is your *best* defense to achieving a workable and safe classroom involvement.

Create Classroom Rules

Classroom rules should be set up on the first day of school. Involve your students in the process. It is very important that they are a part of the decision-making. You can also invite parents to be a part of brainstorming classroom rules simply by sending home a notice inviting them to give you some input to go along with the student's suggestions. When doing this, make sure you send the list of rules the students already suggested. Once the class rules are established, send a revised copy home to the parents for them to sign and return for your file.

Keep in mind that you also want to brainstorm consequences as well from parents.

Implement a Quiet Signal

Every teacher should always have a technique to quiet their students. Quiet signals can be as simple as a "give me five" finger sign, closing your hand and bringing it to the side, ringing or tapping a bell, using a dog clicker, turning on soft music, singing a song, turning off the lights, or just clapping your hands five times. Whatever you do, make sure that it will get the students' attention in three to five seconds. In addition, rehearse the signals daily until all students know its sound and meaning. Also, have consequences for students who do not respond the very first time.

Implement a Stop Strategy

Using a traffic signal light is an excellent tool to use when redirecting class behavior. Give consequences when the whole class has caused the traffic signal light to be set to red. Keep in mind that all consequences should be set prior to using the one-two-three "stop" red light.

Raffle Ticket Strategy

Students love raffle tickets. At the beginning, give students three raffle tickets. Let them know that they cannot write their names on their tickets until the end of the day because if they break a rule or do not follow the procedures, a ticket will be taken away.

When setting up this strategy, brainstorm with your students consequences and rewards and the number of tickets given for following the rules and procedures all day. Award a ticket when you see a student following rules and procedures any time during the day. However, take away a ticket when a student is caught not following rules and procedures. Also, give tickets for class participation, not speaking out loud, being a good listener, etc.

Following-Direction Ticket	Following-Direction Ticket	Following-Direction Ticket	Following-Direction Ticket	Following-Direction Ticket

Using tickets is a great way to give instant incentives. However, you should still find a way to keep track of students' disruption by using a checklist that is based on your rules.

What Are You Thinking? Don't Put Them Down! Don't Criticize!

Try to avoid criticizing your students because it only provokes hostility as well as being damaging to a student's self-esteem. If your criticism is positive and supporting, students will most likely react favorably to your suggestions.

Ellis, Hart, and Small-McGinley (1998) completed a research study on difficult students in the classroom. In the study, the research work was focused on junior high students in an alternative education program for adolescents with a history of behavioral difficulties in school. Students in the research project ranged from ages thirteen years to fifteen years old. Each student was interviewed with unstructured and open-ended questions. Students were asked to think back on their experiences in elementary school and to put together suggestions they would offer to student teachers or beginning teachers about how to make the classroom a more cooperative place for all students to learn. In fact, the research states the following:

> Students did not feel respected by teachers. A teacher who respects students is respected in return and thereby gains much more cooperation and goodwill from students. (Ellis, Hare, & Small-McGinley, 1998)

In fact, throughout my experiences as a classroom teacher, students do show respect only if they receive respect with a caring attitude from their teacher. This is why teachers should model how they expect their students to act. Also, they should talk with their students to get to know them and understand what they are going through. Then provide encouragement, support their learning needs, and make learning enjoyable and not boring.

Based on students' conversations during the research, it was determined that students need to have a sense of belongingness in the classroom. In fact, one student stated that if students don't feel like part of the class, they are not going to want to learn or do what is required of them. On the other hand, if students feel like part of the class, they will probably feel that the teacher cares about them and that the other students like them. Therefore, they will be compelled to do classwork, which is required, and will not cause any discipline problems in the classroom (Ellis, Hart, & Small-McGinley, 1998). Research also indicated that if students do not feel like part of the class, students will in turn resent being at school because they need to have a sense of being a part of the group, and their lack of emotional nurturance outside of school can lead to behavior problems in the classroom, which may in fact lessen their opportunities for experiencing classroom inclusion. In addition, teachers who yell at students around their peers make them feel belittled and embarrassed. As a result, students have to face ridicule from their classmates and, for this reason, carry the anger home to act out negative feelings accordingly. In any event, confronting, accusing, or criticizing a student in front of the class peers can easily cause continuous classroom disruptions of outburst behaviors (Ellis, Hart, & Small-McGinley, 1998).

Keep in mind, when reprimanding a student, think about how you would feel if it were you being criticized or yelled at in front of your colleagues. So respect the student by removing him/her from the area of others and privately redirect the behavior.

When Am I Going to Get Paid?

Students should always be rewarded for their efforts and for reaching goals. However, for the rules to be meaningful, it is important to base the rewards on classroom-set rules. Some students need intrinsic rewards, which are the inner satisfaction of doing well or doing the right thing, such as praise, a handshake, a smile, a wink of the eye, or simply saying, "Very good job." Whereas students who are extrinsic need rewards for good behavior.

So here is a list of free websites where you can get free reward ideas for your class:

- http://www.educationworld.com/_curr/curr301.shtml
- http://www.interventioncentral.org/htmdocs/interventions/rewards/jackpot.php
- http://www.svusd.k12.ca.us/healthykids/PDF/IdeasforRewards.pdf
- http://www.proteacher.com/030000.shtml
- https://www.thoughtco.com/a-point-system-for-reinforcement-3110505

- http://www.theteachersguide.com/ClassManagement.htm
- https://www.aaeteachers.org/index.php/blog/1814-simple-and-free-class-rewards
- http://www.teacherslovelists.com/free-classroom-rewards/

Chapter Seven

Models of Discipline

Canter Model

Lee Canter's theory primarily focuses on the concept of teachers having rights in the classroom. Canter's methods provide an effort to explain to teachers how to observe their rights, as well as the student's rights, and how to take charge of their classroom. For example, all students have the right to know what teachers expect without trying to guess, and teachers have the right to have the support of the parents and administrators.

Although Canter's methods of discipline are unique, he points out that an assertive teacher should always establish rules that apply to appropriate and inappropriate student behaviors. Also, students who follow the rules receive positive consequences. I suggest free time, special privileges, tangible rewards, positive phone calls or emails to parents, eating lunch with the teacher or sitting at the teacher's desk for the day, etc. On the other hand, students who refuse to comply with the rules receive unfavorable consequences such as time away from the group, a parent phone call or email, teacher conference, and the student writing a reflection paper. Canter emphasizes the importance of the consequences being unpleasant but not harmful to the students and always giving students a way out just in case they choose to avoid the class rules consequences (Canter, 1996).

According to research, the Canter model intends to promote a supportive classroom environment that gives teachers the opportunity to teach and students the opportunity to learn. Through this model, students are taught appropriate classroom behavior and teachers are taught to be less punitive in how they discipline students. In fact, this model uses extensive praise and rewards that inhibit more intrinsic motivation (Canter, 1996). Contrary to Glasser's techniques, Canter relies a great deal upon external rewards and control rather than internal rewards to motivate student behaviors (Wikipedia, 2001).

Keep in mind that assertive teachers model responsible behavior and expect the same from their students. They believe that all students can behave if they want and that proper behavior is a student's choice. They do not threaten but enforce the consequences, and lastly, assertive teachers are consistent and follow through with their actions (Moore, 1998).

Glasser Model

The Glasser model supports the fact that students are reasonable beings. He was the first to contend that all students are in control of their behavior, that nothing is forcing them to act a certain way, and that they choose to behave as they do. According to research, the model states that misbehavior is a result of bad choices, while good behavior results from good choices. In other words, if students choose their behaviors, they can also choose to be good or be bad. Therefore, the Glasser model allows the teacher to structure the environment to help students make better choices, and reality therapy helps provide this structure.

The function of the reality therapy in relationship to the classroom is a continuous process made up of two major means (Wikipedia, 2008), which are as follows:

The teacher needs to create a trusting learning environment and use strategies that help students discover what they really want. Then, they should reflect on what students are presently doing. Lastly, they should create a new plan for fulfilling what they want more effectively in the future.

Kounin Model

The Kounin model addresses three approaches. The first is the *ripple effect*; this is when the teacher corrects students' behavior, which often triggers inappropriate behavior from other students who are sitting near the student who showed inappropriate behavior. Also, it is important to identify to students what is wrong with their behavior and what the students should be doing to correct the behavior. Kounin believes that stating very clearly and precisely with firmness is very necessary when implementing the ripple effect to disruptive students. However, with students who become confrontational, their behavior should be immediately directed to the school administrators.

Secondly, Kounin explores the importance of the teacher being eye conscious. In this approach, the teacher has the ability to know what is going on in the classroom by scanning the class perimeter for any students who are about to start a class disruption or students not on task.

Lastly, a teacher can overlap by doing two things at one time. This is what Kounin calls overlapping. For example, when a teacher is teaching a small group and other students are working in other small groups, the teacher can observe and listen to the students in their small group and observe and correct students' behavior in other small groups in different areas of the classroom.

Through the Kounin model, teachers can manage classroom behavior by movement and keeping students alert by holding their attention through active activities and random or blending responses (Kounin, 1970).

Behavior Modification

Behavior modification is a technique of altering an individual's behaviors and reactions to stimuli through positive and negative reinforcement (Wikipedia, 2009).

Kazdin (1982) supports the fact that behavior can be changed if the outcome of the consequences were to influence the behavior. So applying behavior modification in your classroom would certainly discourage inappropriate behavior and encourage positive behavior in students. Using tokens in behavior modification is called reinforcement. Students are given tokens for demonstrating positive classroom behavior, good work, class participation, or following directions. Examples of token reinforcement are plastic chips, play money, tickets, points, or just about anything that the teacher desires.

Go to the following websites for free token ideals:

- http://mspowell.com/tokensystem.html
- http://www.educationworld.com/a_curr/profdev/profdev115.shtml
- http://ng3.ads.warnerbros.com/papermate/cmp/coupons.htm
- http://specialchildren.about.com/od/behaviorstrategies/ss/coupons_6.htm
- http://parenting.leehansen.com/Printables/School/teacher-coupons.htm

The following are other helpful behavior modification sites:

- https://www.teachervision.com/teaching-strategies/behavior-management
- http://www.noogenesis.com/malama/discouragement/Dreikurs/could_it_be_that.html
- http://www.positivediscipline.com
- http://www.nncc.org/Guidance/sac33_behav.mgmt.stress.html

- http://home1.gte.net/stoptc/adolescents.htm
- http://www.dyscalculia.org/ADHD.htm
- http://www.humboldt.edu/~tha1/disciplin.html
- http://www.theteachersguide.com/classroommanagement.htm
- https://www.internet4classrooms.com/teacher.htm
- http://www.nea.org/tools/51721.htm
- https://www.edutopia.org/blog/5-priorities-classroom-management-ben-johnson

Logical Consequences Model

This discipline model was originated by Rudolf Dreikurs in 1974. The approach emphasizes that students should be taught to be responsible for their behavior and that setting up classroom rules and consequences should be decided by the whole class. Dreikurs further states that students want to belong and gain acceptance from their peers and teachers, and if they cannot achieve this, their behavior is directed toward accomplishing this goal by acting out. Dreikurs suggests steps to consider, which are to stop the misbehavior, provide an action that recalls children to the rules, reinstate the limits, and teach alternative behaviors (Dreikurs, Grunwald, & Pepper, 1982).

When using the logical consequences model, keep in mind that the strategy seeks to help students learn from their mistakes. So when implementing consequences, do it with respect and firmness because students are quicker to learn from their mistakes if it is brought to their attention with respect and a firm, direct voice approach. Just remember to give a consequence that will fit the inappropriate behavior. For example, if students are yawning out loud in the classroom, let the students know that yawning out loud is not appropriate for indoor classroom behavior, and to avoid yawning out loud, they should just take a deep breath when feeling the need to yawn. This will help the students not to yawn out loud and control their behavior. On the other hand, if you approach the same behavior by telling the student, "I told you not to yawn out loud in class!" here you have not given a reason or another alternative for the students to change the behavior; therefore, the same behavior will occur again. This kind of behavior reflects what Dreikurs says that students will do what it takes to be accepted and get the attention they need. So the best strategy is to give them logical consequences that will teach them to evaluate situations, learn from their experiences, and allow them to make responsible choices (Dreikurs, Grunwald, & Pepper, 1982).

Teacher Effectiveness Training

Teacher effectiveness training (TET) is an effective behavior modification model for high school classrooms (Edwards, 1997; Wolfgang & Glickman, 1986). This model is also referred to as discipline through developing self-control (Charles, 1996; Gordon, 1989). Also, the TET model contains some of the same characteristics as the social discipline model of Driekurs. What I like about this model is that its specific, primary focus is for teachers to abstain from the use of power methods that promote resistance, rebellion, and blaming. Instead, this model promotes teachers to be more flexible, helping students make decisions that affect their own sense of self-control. Also, it suggests that to influence the student is better than maintaining discipline in the classroom by force. By doing this, teachers should work with students to determine what is creating the inappropriate behavior, and then the teacher can work with the student toward creating positive solutions. As a result, students learn to take control of their problems by finding solutions before their problems become discipline problems.

According to research, group discussions provide teachers with an opportunity to help the children understand themselves and to change their concept of themselves and others, which will eventually change their motivations from hostile to cooperative behavior or living (Dreikurs, 1972, p. 79).

Therefore, at least once a week, having a classroom meeting will create a context for developing empathy and group membership. Jane Nelsen (2006), a Dreikurs-Adlerian writer, suggests eight building blocks for carrying out effective classroom meetings:

1. Form a circle.
2. Practice compliments and appreciation.
3. Create an agenda.
4. Develop communication skills.
5. Learn about separate realities.
6. Recognize the four purposes of behavior.
7. Practice role-playing and brainstorming.
8. Focus on nonpunitive solutions

Lastly, Wolfgang (2001, p. 121) explains, "In a case study, teachers are dealing with a more difficult task. Students who feel hurt and wish to retaliate must be handled in a caring, affectionate manner. It is likely that these students appear unloving and uncaring, and are very hard to warm up to. But this is exactly what the students need to feel, which is 'cared for.'" Look at these techniques that will help you confront situations with students who are seeking power and/or revenge:

- Make a graceful exit.
- Acknowledge the student's power.
- Remove students from the audience.
- Talk about the behavior.
- Use time-out.
- Set the consequence.

> Establishing classroom rules and procedures gives students a sense of security. Students need routines and an action plan to stay on task all through the day.
>
> —Dr. Mavis Bouie

CHAPTER EIGHT

Nonverbal Messages

Nonverbal communication has been defined as communication without words. It includes behaviors such as facial expressions, eyes, touch, tone of voice, and less obvious messages, which include dress and posture. In fact, nonverbal expression can transmit communication that is capable of reinforcing or simply revising or even saying the opposite of what the verbal messages are implying. For example, a smile can indicate "Hello" or "I am pleased with what you are doing." In any event, based on what we are saying, nonverbal communication can be interpreted to whatever message we perceive through some sort of physical movement or attitudes. Research says the ability to understand and use nonverbal communication is an influential tool that will help you connect with others, express what you really mean, plot routes to difficult situations, and build better relationships at home and work (Help Guide, 2008).

Teachers and students are known to use nonverbal expressions all the time. According to research, effective teaching requires that teachers direct as much as their verbal language to student-teacher communication by carefully choosing words that help build a positive and productive classroom environment As a result, the way teachers deliver verbal messages may also contribute much more to students' understanding than the words themselves, especially for children over the age of eight. Research says that young children focus on words the teacher uses; older children focus more on adult's nonverbal behaviors when trying to understand what is expected of them (Mayo & LaFrance, 1978).

It is important for teachers to be aware of the impact nonverbal expressions have on students. So here are some ideas for using nonverbal communication in the classroom that would help improve your effectiveness in a workable classroom environment.

- Proactively use eye contact. Before you start to lecture, make sure you get all students' attention by requesting that they look at your eyes.
- Always make eye contact with students who are fidgety and appear to start getting bored or getting off task with classwork.
- Practice with students making eye contact with the speaker and discuss its importance.

Keep in mind that when you make eye contact with your students, they perceive that what you are saying is of the uttermost importance (Hodge, 1971).

Nonverbal Signals

At the beginning of the school year, it is very important to teach nonverbal signals, such as flicking the lights means it's time to be quiet or clapping the hands five time means to stop what you are doing, stop talking, look, and listen to what is being said by the teacher. Continuously, practice nonverbal signals with your students throughout the school year so that the students will know what they mean when you send out nonverbal messages to correct undesirable classroom behaviors.

Facial Expression

Your facial expressions are personal powerful tools you use every day in the classroom. These expressions can be a simple smile, wink, long stare, frown, or tightening of lips. Facial expressions can project a sense of confidence or persuasion or encourage empowerment in a student's academic ability to succeed. Whatever the reasons, using facial expressions tends to enhance students' academic abilities to successfully succeed without feeling anxiety. For example, when calling on students to respond to questions, try smiling. When a student sees a smile, he/she will not feel threatened by teacher authority. The student will feel that it is okay if mistakes are made. If the student answer the question incorrectly, go back and help the student answer the question correctly simply by prompting and probing until the student gives you the correct answer to the question. Stay positive and calm by showing an "I am pleased with you trying" facial expression. Always praise students during the process. Encouragement is very important for a student's self-esteem and efforts.

Body Language

Movement with the arms, head, hands, and other body parts are pervasive nonverbal communicators. Research has shown that body language has 135 distinct gestures and expressions of the face, head, and body. Of these 135 gestures and expressions, 80 are facial and head gestures that include nine different ways of smiling. Therefore, when you use gestures, be sure to know what they mean because it may mean one thing in one country and something else in another country. For example, the hand signal "okay" and the peace sign is an obscene gesture in other countries, but in the United States, the word *okay* means "fine" or "all right" and the peace sign means "goodbye" or "see you later" (Communication, 2001).

The friendliness of the teacher's body language toward students is revealed by establishing good examples, and it also shortens the teacher-student separation by which a more harmonious learning environment is created. As a matter of fact, the teacher's friendly appearance can greatly encourage the student's learning enthusiasm. As a result, the student's awareness is provoked, and the effect of teaching is greatly improved (Lei, 2006). The following are examples of body language that I find most helpful in the classroom:

- Clap hands to get attention.
- Raise hands and bring them down to indicate, "Sit down."
- Raise hands up to indicate, "Stand up."
- Clap hands, point to students who are acting inappropriately, and direct students to what you want them to do.
- Clap to get attention and tap all fingers on right hand once to indicate, "Stop talking."
- Clap hands and place a finger on lips to indicate, "Stop talking."
- Clap hands and point to eyes to indicate, "Watch the speaker."
- Clap hands and point to ears to indicate, "Listen to the speaker."
- A touch on the student's shoulder or on the student's head indicates approval. However, this is only appropriate for students in grades prekindergarten through grade 3. For students in grades 4 and above, touching should be avoided because students might translate your behavior out of content. So I would suggest a handshake. On the other hand, in grades 6 through 12, I believe that it is unwise for teachers of the opposite sex to touch students, for it can sometimes be misinterpreted. Keeping this in mind, try to use better judgment when communicating by touch with older students or with students of the opposite sex.

The Body Talks
Body language tells how you feel and think.
It expresses feelings of all emotions in many ways.
Students read the teacher's body languages
throughout the day and
Sometimes convey their responses in unacceptable ways.
—Dr. Mavis Bouie

Chapter Nine

Parents, I Need Your Help!

According to the research, parents becoming more involved in their child's school life is a plus for many teachers. Having the support of the parents enables the teachers to focus more on curriculum and less on classroom management (Berla, N., 1992). Therefore, when looking at parental support, teachers should keep in mind that every parent expects their children to be successful in school. They expect their children to also be respectful to their teachers, peers, and other school faculty and staff, as well as behaved. At some point in time, you might have parents who say, "I can't believe my child acted that way. He/she doesn't do that at home. What did the teacher do to cause my child to act that way?" or biggies who say, "That teacher just doesn't like my child. Those teachers are always picking on my child." I know that at least one of these sounds familiar to you. In fact, too often I hear teachers discussing and are frustrated about nonparental school support. Teachers are at their wits' end. Well, teachers, worry no more; these are some suggestions that really work:

Classroom Strategies

- Write a classroom newsletter, including "Super Week Behavior" on students who have good classroom behavior for the week. In the newsletter, comment on parental support.

- Mail a special invitation to invite parents to spend an hour or two with their student in class during center time, reading, or during a special project.
- Phone parents to report good news about their child's progress at least twice a week. This will strengthen teacher-parent relationship.
- Do home visits, done either before or after the school year begins.
- Invite parents to read to the class. For parents who are bilingual, have them read a storybook in their language, and have their child interpret to the class in English.
- Use school agendas for daily communication.
- Have a conference with parents on the first week of school on the phone or in person. In person is better.
- Conduct a personal information session with parents. Include ideas about teaching their children at home and work habits at school that would encourage good classroom behavior.
- An excellent strategy for older students would include parents visiting their child's classroom unexpectedly once every two to three weeks. These visits should not only be when parents are contacted because of a student's misconduct. The teachers should phone parents to make personal invitations to the class. Research states that if parents do not feel welcome at their child's school, there will be less parental involvement (Berla, 1992).
- Classroom tutoring is an excellent way to get parents involved and give them the opportunity to observe their child's work habits.
- Nip parental concerns in the bud before they escalate. Conference as soon as possible, and the two of you should come up with a plan.
- Get discipline ideas from parents about their children. Include ideas in a discipline plan designed for students. Then have the parent(s), the student, and teacher(s) sign and add the date.

Always follow up with conferences in person or on the phone. In person is better.
- Set student expectations with that parent(s), student, and teacher(s) in a face-to-face conference.
- Assign student and parental projects three times a year. Have parents and students report on project together.
- Stay in touch with parents through email whether there are problems or not. Internet correspondence is an excellent tool to send home newsletters, notes, or conference messages.
- Always be professional with parents. You want them to look at you as an expert in your field. So brainstorm ways in which parents feel they can be an asset to their child's education in school and at home. Help the parents set up schedules of learning activities for home use over the weekends, school breaks, and holidays. You want your parents to understand that their child's learning should be an ongoing process to achieve academic success.
- Making the parents feel that their inputs are vital to the academic purpose of what you have planned for their child in your classroom will make your year a productive one and give the students a classroom that is conducive to a workable environment.

Chapter Ten

Management Course of Action

To be an effective classroom teacher, it is important to have effective classroom management strategies. The subtitles in the previous chapters have basically been based on education theories and research of management scholars. In fact, when you look at it, the best way to learn how to manage a classroom is based on personal experiences. Therefore, the following strategies for managing a classroom are tested teacher suggestions taken from various teachers over fourteen years.

Strategies

- *Arrive early.* Always arrive early for school. If you are on time for work, you can get the last-minute things needed to begin class on time. Also, you have time to review notes and emails from administrators.
- *Get organized.* At the end of the day, have students' morning works placed on their desks, extra pencils sharpened, and for those teachers who have students stack their chairs at the end of the day, students who arrive to class early have them to place chairs under students' desks before they arrive. You want to have everything in order so when students enter your classroom, all they need to do is sharpen their pencil and

begin morning assignments. It is very important to have a structured morning. Students need to know exactly what is expected of them as soon as they enter the classroom.

- *Start class on time.* When the bell rings, meet and greet your students at the door. Require that all talking stops as they enter, set a timer for fifteen minutes, and let students know that the timer is set and that they should have their pencils sharpened and be seated and working before the timer bell rings. For students who are late to class, set the timer at five minutes to begin their work.
- *Have enough morning assignments.* Morning assignments should be automatic and routine. Make sure that you have enough morning work for all students that would take at least thirty minutes of the first half of the class. You want the work to last after morning announcements.
- *Early finishers.* Have folders set up for all students for any incomplete assignments and folders with extra work.
- *Set up dismissal procedures.* Assign certain students to pick up papers and check centers for neatness. Require that all students are in their seats and are quiet before dismissal announcements.
- *Housekeeping.* Select a day and time to clean up. Require students to clean out their desk. This is important for organization.
- *Review classroom rules and procedures.* Once a week, review rules and procedures. Keep reinforcing them all year, and you will see less behavior problems.
- *Inappropriate behavior.* As soon as you notice inappropriate behaviors, stop it without distracting the other students. Walk over to the students, whisper in the students' ears, "Stop it and get back to work," or walk over to the students, get eye contact, and shake your head no and point to their work.
- *Assignment transitions.* Classroom movement should be done as quickly as possible. If you have centers, make sure that they are in areas of the classroom where students can move

quickly to. Placing centers in corner areas are great because students will have room to work in the center area of the classroom. Have activities instructions written down in each center. Students need to know what they are going to do before they start activities. Always assign a group captain that will be able to assist students when needed.

- *Use eye contact.* When lecturing to the students, always make eye contact. Never turn your back when talking to your students.
- *Set high expectations.* Let students know what you expect of them, and let them know that they will have consequences if they do not follow classroom rules and procedures.
- *Positive role model.* Always be polite to your students. Let them know that you are going to respect them and expect them to respect you. Never use sarcasm when telling students what you expect them to do.
- *Consistency and firmness.* Whenever students break rules, always follow through with established consequences. Communicate directly to the students who are breaking the rules, and do not punish all the students for one student's mistake.
- *Do not make threats.* Never threaten students or make promises. When rules are broken, act immediately.
- *Use body language or nonverbal signals.* Always use nonverbal messages to stop or prevent inappropriate behavior immediately.
- *Drop a book, switch off lights, ring a bell, sing a tune, and turn on music.* These are strategies that will help get students back on track when they are all talking at the same time.
- *Please help me behave.* Let your students know that you want to help them behave. Once a week, have a class group meet to discuss ways on controlling anger and brainstorm ways to develop their own self-discipline.
- *Corporal punishment.* Never ever use corporal punishment! Whenever students are totally out of control, contact the office immediately for assistance and contact the parent.

- *Lesson plans.* Make sure that your lessons are well planned. Every activity should involve all students. All activities should be differentiated to meet the need of every student. Center activities are an excellent place to have a variety of activities to meet every student's learning need.
- *Compliment students.* Everyone loves to be complimented, so praise your students even when they seem to be off task. You would be surprised how just kind words—for example, "I like the way all the guys are working"—will automatically get students who are off task back on task.
- *Call parents.* Involving parents is the best discipline defense a teacher could possibly have. Let the parents know when their child is not following school and classroom rules and procedures. Do not wait until problems escalate. Parents will want to know before the problem gets worse. Always talk in person. Phone calls are okay, but you want the parent to know that you care and want the best for their child. Parents need to see your concern, not just hear it. Once you have convinced parents of your concern for their children, they will work with you until the end.
- *Celebrate.* At the end of the week, always celebrate with your class. You can give a popcorn party, twenty minutes of free time, recess, art project, permission to talk with their friends in class, extra center time, or permission to sit outside and read a book. We all want to get paid for working hard.

These guidelines are only a few that I find very helpful and that result in an unproblematic running classroom. Therefore, if you will incorporate the above classroom management strategies, you will prevent the minority of the discipline problems that is preventing your class from becoming a workable environment.

Remember to always do the following:

- Teach and enforce expected behaviors.
- Be consistent.

- Be prepared.
- Be realistic.
- Be the motivator.
- Give praise.

The following are great websites for classroom management on the first week of school:

- https://www.smartclassroommanagement.com/2010/07/24/classroom-management-strategy-first-days-of-school/
- https://www.centervention.com/classroom-management-plan/
- http://teacher.scholastic.com/professional/classmgmt/bully_free.htm
- http://www.proteacher.com/030000.shtml
- http://712educators.about.com/od/classroomhelpers/Classroom_Management_Tools.htm
- https://www.thereligionteacher.com/classroom-management-strategies-first-weeks-of-schooll/

Children are our greatest investment. We only have one time to get it right. So let's not miss the opportunity to make a positive difference in their lives.

—Dr. Mavis Bouie

CHAPTER ELEVEN

Preschool, Two- to Four-Year-Olds

Anything Could Happen

My encounter with working with prekindergarten children was one of the most interesting experiences of my teaching career because pre-K students are one of the most manipulative children I have ever taught. When working with this age group, know that children have already figured out how they are going to run the classroom because in reality, classroom boundaries are unlimited to them and the teacher is the stranger who is entering their world of fun, games, and discovery. So when establishing a prekindergarten classroom, keep in mind that these students will either accept you or reject you within the first two days or week of class. But if you can make it through the first week or two, you might have a chance of surviving only if you have taken control on the first day of school. Just keep in mind that the first week of school is imperative on learning through observation what kind of children you are teaching. In other words, learning the personality of each child is crucial to effective classroom management.

Classroom leaders are very important; therefore, use the first two weeks to discover who the leaders are. Usually, class leaders will not expose themselves on the first day or two of class. However, after the first week, the head honchos of the class will surface. Keep in mind that class leaders are not always children who show excellent conduct.

Signs of Manipulations When Identifying the Class Leaders

- Very helpful, wants attention, and will do whatever it takes to get it
- Enjoyable, delightful attitude, with bossy behavior to peers
- Always verbalizing feelings about self and others
- Not afraid to act like the person in charge
- Models teacher's behavior when speaking to other students
- Talkative and sometimes disregards teacher when asked to stop talking
- At times models to children unacceptable class behavior
- Might move from the proximity of the teacher

Setting Consequences

Setting consequences for inappropriate behavior should be established by the teacher and students. When setting consequences, prompt children in the directions you want them to go, for example:

- Time-out.
- Talk with the teacher.
- Talk with the teacher and parent.

Children need to become aware that their inappropriate behavior has drawbacks. So keep in mind to first redirect the child's behavior before reprimanding it. Use strategies such as saying the following:

- I like the way _____ is helping in housekeeping.
- _____ is doing a great job sitting quietly on the carpet.
- Wow! _____ is a great listener.
- Let all of us put on our listening ears. Don't let them fall off. Lock them tightly.

Handling Tantrums

Children's tantrums can be caused by many things, such as attention deficit disorder and other biological factors that cause impulsive behaviors that are uncontrolled by the child. Also, children may be emotionally attached to objects the teacher is unaware of, and at that moment of outburst, they may feel the need for that object. Sometimes young children don't know how to express the need for the things that make them feel secure. It may appear that the child is crying to have their way, but they are expressing in a more aggressive behavior to have their needs met at that moment.

Therefore, when handling tantrums, it might be best things to do the following:

- Let it play out until the child stops.
- Don't tell the child to stop because the child will escalate the behavior.
- Redirect the child's attention to something that is a favorite.
- Whisper in the child's ear, "I understand how you feel, but I need you to stop crying and help me after the lesson."

Oppositional Behavior

This is another factor that causes the child to become angry, defiant, annoying, noncompliant, and sometimes aggressive. In order to diagnose this kind of behavior, it must occur more than six consecutive months (American Psychiatric Association, 2000).

Research implies that parents tend to tolerate their child's oppositional behaviors because they feel that the child is limited with the inability to understand consequences of their actions. Therefore, when handling advanced tantrum behaviors, it is imperative to just allow the child to scream and kick it out until the child gets tired (Campbell, 2002). So just continue to do what you are doing because feeding into the behavior is just what the child wants. Although, at the first moment, the child might pause to see your reaction to the inappropriate behavior; at that point, say, "If you are screaming, you can't hear what I am going to tell you. It will make you feel happy again." Then say, "So when you finish crying, let me know, and you and I can sit and talk about why you are not happy and we can do something to make you feel better." Using this strategy approach gives the child options first to think about the behavior, and the disruption will not get the attention he desires at that time.

Nevertheless, don't focus your attention on the tantrum but on the child. Once the loud crying starts diminishing, say to the child, "Thank you for not crying so loud. Now you are really acting like a big boy or big girl. I love big boys or big girls because I need them to be the teacher's helpers." Now, you are shifting the responsibility of being a leader by letting the child know that leaders must act a certain way. Once the child stops, give he or she strategies to redirect inappropriate behaviors to prevent future outbursts, such as the following:

- When feeling sad, tell the teacher you are sad and why.
- Sing a song instead of crying when you are sad.
- Ask for paper to draw a picture of why you are sad.
- Ask to color pictures in a big coloring book.
- Put a puzzle together.
- Play a game on the computer or iPad.
- Ask for a hug.
- Ask for permission to put your head down and take a nap.
- Read or look at favorite picture books.
- Create something with Play-Doh.

These are only suggestions that work for this age group. However, it is always suggested to get feedback from parents or guardians on some of the strategies used at home that works.

With regard to research, a substantial percentage of children will outgrow some behavioral problems. In fact, longitude studies suggested that 50 to 60 percent of children showing high rates of disruptive behaviors at ages three to four years old will continue to show tantrums at school age. Also, inappropriate behaviors are influenced by the child's biological and environmental factors, which are manifested in their characteristics and may stem from the home environment. In other words, parental environment and genetics are factors that play a part during the child's developmental stages of the child's characteristic development.

Therefore, it is best to familiarize yourself with basic elements of a child's behaviors before indulging with teaching an activity or skill. Suggested strategies are the following:

1. *Set perimeters.* Let the children know that you are the adult and you have established rules of the classroom. However, you would like for them to help you add two or three more rules for the class to follow.

    This strategy makes the children a part of the decision-making process as well as gives the teacher the opportunity to introduce them to classroom rules, consequences, and expectations.

2. *Give reminders.* During instructional activities, keep praising children who are being cooperative and are modeling good conduct and listening skills. Select a child or two to praise with smiles, claps, something from a treasure box, etc.

3. *Encouragement.* Use a variety of behavior incentives to encourage good classroom behaviors. Also, get suggestions from each child's parent and ask for stickers and healthy treats (no peanut products or toys that can be put into the child's mouth, nose, or ears).

Teacher-and-Student Conference

It is essential for teachers to confer with the child immediately when classroom behavior is inappropriately displayed. Keep in mind that when working with pre-Ks, the teacher must be direct and always reinforce structured boundaries. Children at any age need rules and limitations of their actions. Believe it or not, they do want and need structure indirectly and directly to feel safe at all times.

Tips to Achieve an Enriched Classroom Environment

1. Always show love and not anger. Children at any age group read facial expressions. They have an innate radar that can detect if they have pushed a nerve. In fact, your reactions let them know that they have weakened you to the extent that you will give in to their behavior. Also, they will go as far as to ask you, "Are you upset or mad at me?"
2. Always play it cool by taking deep breaths, counting, singing, humming out loud, or just laughing at them with a smile. Just keep smiling and start singing, "If You're Happy and You Know It." Once you start to sing, the class will start singing along. This strategy will redirect unwanted behaviors to a more positive approach and pleasant classroom environment. In fact, I call this strategy the transmit approach to positive behavior.
3. Include classroom rules in your morning meetings daily. Let the children know that unacceptable behavior will not get them what they want, but acceptable behavior will get them the things they want. Give examples to the children.
4. When a rule is broken or unacceptable behavior is noticed, let it be known to the child or children immediately. However, give the child or children a chance to redeem themselves by giving them warnings. Allow the student(s) to respond to

How To Achieve a Workable Classroom Environment   71

three warnings. After each warning, let the student(s) know that you are giving them a chance to correct their behavior. When speaking to the child or children, always use direct eye contact and direct tone of voice by dropping your voice one octave lower.

Let the child or children know that you are displeased with the behavior and ask them what they can do to act better. Always redirect the behavior solution back to the child or children. Once they give you a response, have them illustrate a picture at their tables and share it with you. This will give you (the teacher) the opportunity to individually speak with each child about their behavior.

As a teacher, it is always your responsibility to set the stage toward good classroom behavior. So no matter how frustrated you may become, always stay calm and keep an authoritative tone of voice, and always use your eyes to scan the class for children who are off task. A positive teacher model is important because children are always watching you and your reactions. Model to them how to solve problems by thinking out loud. Model steps and remind them of consequences when they misbehave.

NOTES

FREE RESOURCES

For classroom management, go to http://www.proteacher.com/030000.shtmI.

For morning meeting ideas, go to https://mnliteracy.org/sites/default/files/gamesactivitiesbook_0.pdf.

For older students, go to https://www.slideshare.net/MandieFunk/morning-meeting-greetings?next_slideshow=1.

For behavior interventions, go to http://www.interventioncentral.org/behavioral-intervention-modification.

For videos, go to https://www.youtube.com/watch?v=98wLc-Vgjug&feature=youtu.be or https://www.youtube.com/watch?v=ud4y-V9QBzU.

For positive reinforcements for school and home, go to https://www.verywellfamily.com/positive-reinforcements-fix-behavior-problems-2161919.

For free rewards, go to the following:

- http://www.interventioncentral.org/behavioral-interventions/rewards/jackpot-ideas-classroom-rewards
- https://www.teachervision.com/top-10-free-cheap-rewards-students
- http://www.educationworld.com/a_curr/curr301.shtml
- https://www.thoughtco.com/free-and-effective-classroom-rewards-2081550

For RTI interventions resources, go to http://www.interventioncentral.org/behavioral-interventions/rewards/jackpot-ideas-classroom-rewards.

NOTES

Summary

Let's Sum It Up!

I realize that as teachers, we cannot change students or fix all students, but if teachers can help one child, isn't it all worth it? I don't regret becoming a teacher, and I don't think I ever will. However, using the content strategies in this book will help teachers achieve the energy students bring into the room by expanding their mind through strategies that will help them achieve their highest potentials. In addition, students will be able to ask questions without fear of being humiliated by their peers as well as help other students discover ways in which they have control over their behaviors and choices. Implementing the classroom management strategies will help you achieve a workable situation that will make you love your job, make learning fun for the students as well as for the teacher, and diminish some of the problems that you thought would never go away. Then you will say to yourself, "I now have a workable classroom environment that I can handle. This is truly an answer to a prayer."

Notes

APPENDIX

Where do you find information on bullying and cyberbullying in schools?

- For the Professional Misconduct and Discipline complaint hotline, call 1-800-442-8106 *or* email conduct@mail.nysed.gov.
- Delaware Bullying Prevention Association welcomes any questions or comments you might have. All calls will be treated in a confidential manner. Call (302) 778-3908 or email us at info@bullyprevention.org.
- For bright ideas to stop bullying in your classroom, check out these resources:

1. www.cyberbullying.us
2. www.cyberbully411.org
3. www.stopcyberbullying.org
4. http://www.jimwrightonline.com/pdfdocs/bully/bullyBooklet.pdf
5. http://www.internet4classrooms.com/character_ed.htm
6. http://www.teach-nology.com/ideas/bullying/
7. http://pubs.cas.psu.edu/freepubs/pdfs/ui367.pdf
8. http://www2.scholastic.com/browse/article.jsp?id=4099
9. http://www.bam.gov/sub_yourlife/yourlife_bullyroundup.html
10. http://www.pacerkidsagainstbullying.org/
11. http://www.ncpc.org/topics/by-audience/law-enforcement/teaching-children/handouts
12. http://www.stopbullyingnow.hrsa.gov/kids/

Notes

Glossary

behavior. Actions that are observable and explicit.

behavior modification. To manipulate observable behavior by altering the consequences, outcomes, or rewards that follow the behavior.

computer. An electronic machine capable of accepting data, manipulating or performing arithmetic on such data at high speed, and showing or printing the results.

concept. An idea, thought, or opinion that may include objects, events, or a process that can be put into a group with some similarities that have the same common goal.

cooperative learning. Students are grouped in mixed learning abilities, such as high, medium, and low, to work together on an assigned task.

diversity. Occurs when people are from different cultures.

engaged time. The actual time students spend involved in the learning process.

goals. A point or place that one is striving to reach.

instructional strategy. A plan of action that teaches a lesson, unit, or a course that includes a mythology and procedures.

instructional time. Students' class time that is put into productive learning activities.

learning. Because of a student's academic performance and experiences, a permanent change takes place in their lives.

modeling. One who demonstrates or serves as an example to positive behaviors and/or values.

motivation. Manipulating one's desires in a direction that would produce positive actions in their behavior.

nonverbal reinforcement. Using some form of physical action as a positive consequence to strengthen a behavior or event (Moore, 1998, p. 345).

objective. A description of an instructional purpose.

positive reinforcement. Using a stimulus to produce good behavior.

procedure. Series of steps that are mapped out to direct ways to learning objectives.

reinforcement. The use of strengthening a behavior through consequences to attain positive classroom performance.

ripple effect. The imitation of one's behavior from one person to the other.

spare time. Periods of instructional time that is used to focus on leisure activities such as reading a book, working on a crossword puzzle, or playing games on the computer.

time on task. Engaged time that results in performance or achievement of 80 percent or more.

tokens. Rewards such as tickets, chips, pencils, candy, erasers, ink pens, toys, markers, crayons, play coins, or play money.

RESOURCES

Allen, T. (1996). Developing a discipline plan for you. Retrieved April 4, 2009, from http://www.humboldt.edu/~tha1/canter.html

Arthur-Kelly et al. (2006) *Classroom management: Creating positive learning environments* (2nd ed.). Thomson.

Assertive Discipline (2008). In *Wikipedia*. Retrieved May 20, 2009, from http://en.wikipedia.org/wiki/Assertive_discipline

Avalon East School District. (2003). Safe and caring schools' policy. Retrieved May 12, 2009, from http://www.aesd.ca/policy

Barnhart, R. K. (Ed.). (1996). *The world book dictionary.* Chicago, IL: World Book.

Behavior modification (2008). In *Wikipedia*. Retrieved May 24, 2009, from http://en.wikipedia.org/wiki/Reality_Therapy

Benard, B. (1995). Fostering resiliency in urban schools. In B. Williams (Ed.), *Closing the achievement gap: A vision to guide change in beliefs and practice.* Oak Brook, IL: Research for Better Schools and North Central Regional Educational Laboratory.

Berla, N. (1992). Getting middle school parents involved. *Education Digest, 58*(2), 18.

Bossert, S. T. (1979). *Tasks and social relationships in classrooms.* Cambridge, Eng.: Cambridge University Press.

Brehm, S. S. & Kassin, S. M. (1996). *Social psychology.* Boston: Houghton Mifflin.

Brophy, J. E. (1983). Classroom organization and management. *The Elementary School Journal, 83*(4), 265–285.

Brophy, J. E. (1998). *Motivating students to learn.* Boston: McGraw Hill.

Brophy, J. E. & Evertson, C. M. (1976). *Learning from teaching: A developmental perspective.* Boston: Allyn and Bacon.

Burden, P. R. (2003). *Classroom management: Creating a successful learning community* (2nd ed.). Hoboken, NJ: John Wiley.

Canter, L. & Canter, M. (1984). *Assertive discipline: Resource materials workbook elementary, K-6.* Santa Monica, CA: Lee Canter and Associates.

Canter, L. & Canter, M. (1992). *Assertive discipline: Positive behavior management for today's classroom.*

Canter, L. (1987). *Lee Canter's assertive discipline. School wide positive activities ideas for reinforcing positive school wide behavior.* Santa Monica, CA: Lee Canter and Associates

Canter, L. (1996). Discipline alternatives, first, the rapport-then, the rules. *I Learning, 24*(5), 12, 14.

Charles, C. M. (1996). *Building classroom discipline* (5th ed.). White Plains, NY: Longman.

Coleman, G. (2001). *Issues in education: View from the other side.* Westport, CT: Greenwood.

Nonverbal communication. (2001). Retrieved June 2, 2009, from http://coestudents.valdosta.edu/knbennet/nonverbal_communication.htm

Duke, D. L. & Meckel, A. M. (1984). *Teachers' guide to classroom management.* New York: Random House.

Diaz, C. F. (2001). *Multicultural education for the 21st century.* New York: Addison-Wesley.

Doyle, W. (1986). Classroom organization and management. In M. Wittrock (Ed.), *Handbook of Research on Teaching* (3rd ed.). New York: Macmillan.

Doyle, W. (1990). Classroom management techniques. In O. C. Moles (Ed.), *Student Discipline Strategies.* Albany: State University of New York Press.

Doyle, W. & Carter, K. (1984). Academic tasks in classrooms. *Curriculum Inquiry, 14*(2), 129–149.

Dreikurs, R (2004). Encyclopædia Britannica. Retrieved March 7, 2009, from http://www.britannica.com/eb/article?tocId=9031174

Dreikurs, R. & Cassel, P (1972). *Discipline without tears* (2nd ed.) (pp. 1–84). A Plum Book.

Dreikurs, R. & Grey, L (1968). *The new approach to discipline: Logical consequences* (pp. 1–82). A Plum Book.

Dreikurs, R., Grunwald, B. B., & Pepper, F. C. (1982). *Maintaining sanity in the classroom* (2nd ed.). New York: Harper and Row.

Duke, D. (1979). *Classroom management. Yearbook of the national society for the study of education.* Chicago: University of Chicago Press.

Edwards, C. H. (1997). *Classroom discipline and management* (2nd ed.). Upper Saddle River, NJ: Prentice-Hall.

Ellis, W. D. & Kidwell, P. J. (1995). A study of assertive discipline and recommendations for effective classroom management methods. (ERIC document reproduction services No. ED 379 207).

Ellis, J., Hart, S., & Small-McGrinley, J. (1998). The perspectives of "difficult" students on belonging and inclusion in the classroom. *Reclaiming Child and Youth, 7*(3) (pp.142–146). Retrieved May 18, 2009 from http://www.cyc-net.org/cycol-1203-ellis.html

Emmer, E. T., Evertson, C. M, & Anderson, L. M. (1980). Effective classroom management at the beginning of the school year. *The Elementary School Journal, 80*(5), 219–231.

Erlandson, C. (2002). Classroom management: Creating a climate for learning. Retrieved February 9, 2004, from http://www.stf.sk.ca/prof_growth

Evertson, C. M. (1985). Training teachers in classroom management: An experiment in secondary classrooms. *Journal of Educational Research, 79*, 51–58.

Evertson, C. M. (1989). Improving elementary classroom management: A school-based training program for beginning the year. *Journal of Educational Research, 83*, 82–90.

Evertson, C. M. (1997). Classroom management. In H. J. Walberg & G. D. Haertel (Eds.), *Psychology and Educational Practice*. Berkeley: McCutchan.

Evertson, C. M. & Emmer, E. T. (1982). Effective management at the beginning of the school year in junior high classes. *Journal of Educational Psychology, 74*(4), 485–498.

Evertson, C. M. & Harris, A. H. (1992). What we know about managing classrooms. *Educational Leadership, 49*(7), 74–78.

Evertson, C. M. & Harris, A. H. (1999). Support for managing learning-centered classrooms: The classroom organization and management program. In H. J. Freiberg (Ed.), *Beyond Behaviorism: Changing the Classroom Management Paradigm.* Boston: Allyn and Bacon.

Fitzsimmons, M. K. (1998). School-wide behavioral management systems. Retrieved January 12, 2009, from http://library.educationworld.net/a11/a11-158.html

Flint, L. J. (2000). An equation for teacher leadership. Retrieved January 14, 2009, from http://www.virtualflint.com/student/mp/leadershipequation.html

Freiberg, H. J. (1999). *Beyond Behaviorism: Changing the Classroom Management Paradigm.* Boston: Allyn and Bacon.

Freiberg, H. J., Stein, T. A., & Huang, S. (1995). The effects of classroom management intervention on student achievement in inner-city elementary schools. *Educational Research and Evaluation, 1,* 33–66.

Gardner, H. (1993). *Multiple intelligences: The theory in practice.* New York: Basic Books.

Glasser, W. (1977). 10 steps to good discipline. *Today's Education, 66,* 61–63.

Glasser, W. (1965). *Reality therapy: A new approach to psychiatry.* New York: Harper and Row.

Gump, P. V. (1982). School settings and their keeping. In D. Duke (Ed.), *Helping teachers manage classrooms.* Alexandria, VA: Association for Supervision and Curriculum Development.

Hand, M. (2003). Classroom management: Strategies and techniques. Retrieved February 21, 2000, from http://edu.lrrcn.ab.ca/srgloria/school/Administration/Research/classroom_management.htm

Hodge, R. L. (1971). Interpersonal classroom communication through eye contact. *Theory into Practice, 10,* 264–265.

Jackson, L. & Panyan, M. V. (2002). *Positive behavioral support in the classroom: Principles and practices.* Baltimore, Maryland: Brooks.

Jones, V. (1996). Classroom management. In J. Sikula (Ed.), *Handbook of Research on Teacher Education* (2nd ed.). New York: Simon and Schuster.

Jussim, L., & Eccles, J. (1992). Teacher expectations: II. Construction and reflection of student achievement. *Journal of Personality & Social Psychology, 63*(3), 947–961.

Kazdin A. E. (1982). The token economy: A decade later. *Journal of Applied Behavior Analysis, 15*(3), 431–445. doi: 10.1901/jaba.1982.15-431

Kounin, J. S. (1970). *Discipline and group management in classrooms.* New York: Holt, Rinehart and Winston.

Lei, Z (2006). The use of body Language in Middle Schools. Retrieved June 2, 2009, from http://www.englishcn.com/zh/writing/paper/20070806/7076.html

Mayo, C. & Lafrance, M. (1978). On the acquisition of nonverbal communication: A review. *Merrill-Palmer Quarterly* (24), 213–214.

Milner, S. (1995). Discipline in the schools. Retrieved February 9, 2009, from http://www.nstu.ca/issues/issues/AV100sm.html

Moore, K. D. (1998). *Classroom teaching skills* (4th ed.). McGraw-Hill.

Naegle, P. (2002). *Teaching classroom routines and procedures.* Retrieved May 1, 2009, from http://www.2.scholastic.com/browse/article

Newfoundland and Labrador. (2003). Creating a positive school climate. Retrieved February 9, 2009, from http://www.gov.nf.ca/edu/dept/safesch.htm

Nonverbal communication skills: The power of nonverbal communication and body language. (2008). Retrieved May 30, 2009, from http://www.helpguide.org/mental/eq6_nonverbal_communication.htm#nonverbal2

Owens, R. (2001). *Organizational behavior in education* (7th ed.). Toronto: Allyn and Bacon.

Padmanabhan, C. (2009). Sitting in rows is better for primary school kids. Retrieved April 28, 2009, from http://www.pitara.com

Pitner, S. (2008). Positive classroom discipline teacher strategies that encourage responsive students, Retrieved May 3, 2009, from https://www.classroom-management-tips.suite.101.com

Rosa, S. B. (2004). What did you say: Using nonverbal communication to improve teacher effectiveness. Retrieved May 31, 2009, from www.responsiveclassroom.org/PDF_files/feature_33.pdf

Reality Therapy (2008). In *Wikipedia*. Retrieved May 21, 2009, from http://en.wikipedia.org/wiki/Reality_Therapy

Responsible behavior curriculum guide strengthens classroom management skills for beginning teachers. (2009). Retrieved May 4, 2009, from http://www.canter.net

Shore, K. (2006). *Hitting or threatening a teacher,* Retrieved May 4, 2009, from http://www.educationworld.com/a_curr/shore/shore069.shtml

Singh, A. (Ed.). (2001). *Classroom management: A reflective perspective.* New Delhi: Kanishka.

Steere, F. (1988). *Canter's assertive behavior. Becoming an effective classroom manager: A resource for teachers* (pp. 46–50). New York: State University.

Taylor, A. (1996). Understanding children's behavior: The key to effective guidance. Retrieved February 22, 2009, from http://www.cfc-efc.ca/docs/cccf/00009_en.htm

Weade, R. & Evertson, C., M. (1988). The construction of lessons in effective and less effective classrooms. *Teaching and Teacher Education 4*, 189–213.

Wolfgang, C. (1995). *Assertive discipline: Solving discipline problems. Methods and models for today's teachers* (3rd ed.) (pp. 249–267). Needham Heights, MA: Allyn & Bacon.

Wong, H. & Wong, R. (2008). Going beyond folder 12: Students who face the board learn more. 94. Retrieved April 28, 2009, from http: www.effectiveteaching.com

Wolfgang, C. H. (2001). *Solving discipline and classroom management problems: Methods and models for today's teachers* (p. 121). New York: John Wiley and Sons.

Wolfgang, C. H. & Glickman, C. D. (1980). *Solving discipline problems: Strategies for classroom teachers.* Boston, MA: Allyn and Bacon.

Made in the USA
Columbia, SC
15 June 2023